Crossing Spain

wandering in the land of the bull

Alan Passey

(with a spare pair of pants -

and a bike)

Cover design: Alan Passey
Photography: Alan Passey

Disclaimer:
The advice and strategies found within may not be suitable for every situation. This work is sold with the understanding that neither the author nor the publisher are held responsible for the results accrued from the advice in this book.

blog: www.singlemaltmonkey.com

About the Author

Alan Passey keeps the show on the road near Cirencester in the UK where he writes, paints, plays music and dreams of travelling.

For Fi,
for your love and support, and letting me go

Contents

Acknowledgements

Persuaded to commit my experiences to print, I am grateful for the encouragement and proof reading of my friend, neighbour and educationalist, Ann O'Hara, whose grammatical diligence was humbling. If an errant apostrophe has slipped through it is entirely my fault. And to Dr. Bob Reid, who will always tell me straight, hence whose opinion matters. Thanks to Andy Kirk at Performance Cycles, Poulton who sorted me out with the perfect bike fit and Rachael Woodhouse, personal trainer at Fit for Polo, made me feel the pain.

1. Tarmac Envy

Villafruela is a small village approached from the south to a crossroads. No signs. No signals. No sign of life. High up on moorland, not a bar on my phone to be had. An old lady heading towards me taking her morning constitutional, quietly minding her own business to the song of the birds, was about to encounter the 'lost British tourist'.

Choosing to avoid the more direct and, no doubt, less interesting faster carriageway to Burgos, I had worked out my route the previous night, listing the significant points that I would pass through on a scrap of paper, committing many of them to memory, and tucking the paper safely into my pocket.

'Excuse me, which is the way to Iglesiarubia ?' I asked in my best Spanish.

She looked at me incredulously. 'There in the square,' she said pointing over my shoulder. Behind me, rising between the houses, was the centuries old facade of the village church, its imposing bell tower peering over the village rooftops. Only an idiot could miss it. 'No, no,' I said, 'Iglesiarubia'. Iglesiarubia was the next hamlet on my route but no matter how many times I asked the lady the only word she heard was 'iglesia' - church. 'There, dimwit,' I think she said, pointing, her gestures becoming increasingly elaborate with frustration.

Some parts of my brain were scrabbling frantically for the Spanish for 'village'. 'Ah, what is it? What is it?' they panicked. The part of my brain that knew the answer watched this merry dance smugly, refusing to proffer the answer until about 15 minutes later when it was too late. I gave up and thanked her and she sauntered off to tell her friends that she'd met a blind cyclist who couldn't see the church.

I tossed a coin. Tossed again. Best of three. Took a soggy bite out of a floppy banana that had ripened in my back pocket, and best-guessed. Not my favoured approach. I was cycling, after all, and a few miles in the wrong direction is energy wasted. Sometimes you need a little luck.

This had all begun some years ago when my wife and I frequently found ourselves running to the sun for some rest and relaxation in Andalucia. The flights were plentiful and cheap, and at the time of writing still are, and our surroundings, having dropped our bags and stopped the world, were warm and welcoming and serious chilling down could commence.

Exploring in our hire car I became fascinated by the smoothness of the road surface. I could be that sad! It seemed to me that the roads in the UK, pothole fiestas that many were, were a shameful inferior substitute. I dreamed of cycling along these pristine roads, smooth as smooth could be, the sun on my back, my cares and woes a distant memory. I had a bad case of Tarmac Envy.

I enthused to my friends back home that it would be fun to cycle from one end of Spain to the other, coast to coast, but never really gave it much thought beyond that. Unfortunately, I became something of broken record as the years passed and sooner or later I was going to have to shut up or put up. Then I heard of a man in his 70's who sailed around the coast of the UK, even the rough bits, and so that was it. Cycling across Spain had to be easier than that, and if he could rise to the challenge, so could I…

My plans were simply romantic. Dip my toe in the Mediterranean and then head straight for the Atlantic on the north coast. Cycling all the way, travelling alone, with only my enthusiasm and my pidgin Spanish to

8

sustain me. But who am I kidding - it was going to be a hell of a holiday adventure.What follows is an account of my two trips so far with tips and advice based upon my experience and hoping that I can convey the absolute joy of discovering Spain off the beaten track and if you're inclined, on your bike. The planning and the packing, the people and the landscapes. And of course, tarmac envy, cycling Spain is an absolute treat.

If the practicalities of preparation are not your thing then don't feel you have to wade through this part. It will be very much a hands-on 'How to -' bit so feel free to move straight to the journeys and the fun. I won't feel slighted

The Planning

Firstly, let me make it clear that I didn't want a trip lugging tents and pots and pans strapped to both wheels. This made me something of a curio upon arriving in Santander at the end of my first ride. 'Is that it? Is that all you've got?' asked another elderly adventurer, who, worryingly, had a cuddly mascot strapped to his handlebars. I would also learn that besides a tent and other camping equipment he was carrying a kettle, his favourite china cup, tea of course, and his laptop. He was certainly not interested in Dave Brailsford's marginal gains.[1]

Another tourer boasted that his bike weighed in at well over 40 kilos of extra baggage. I grinned in wonder. What on earth for, I thought? Oh well, each to their own. But that's not for me.

---

[1] Sir David Brailsford is currently General Manager of Team Sky professional cycling team and champions the philosophy of "marginal gains".A practice of reducing component values by 1% to gain cumulative enhancements in performance.

I wanted, as far as possible, to replicate cycling at home. Get my gear on, fill my water bottles, jump on and ride. This meant carrying the bare minimum and arranging beds for the night. Therefore, planning the route required some careful attention and became part of the adventure. As the route developed, the anticipation grew. Not that I'm an adventurer by any means, but Captain Cook never had it this easy. Google maps, Google Earth, web images and all the hotel and b'n'b booking sites made putting this sort of trip together easier than could be imagined even 30 years ago.

My maxim was 'don't strain the bike, don't strain the legs, and we'll all get through safely enough'. All - me and my bike. It's funny how, when locked into a solo adventure, your bike takes on the role of your best friend and travelling companion. I got to know my bike very well and would often offer encouragement when climbing hills. Perhaps I was on the road alone too long. However, I digress.

By my reckoning I was about to cycle 700 miles or more and everything needed to be up to scratch before I left. That included me and I thought it would be money and time well spent to have a professional bike fit. The perfect pain free position, I figured, would be a good idea.I booked my bike in for a strip-down service with my local cycle shop and so spruced up with all new consumable parts the bike was ready to break down again for packing. New cleats on my shoes were also a must.

If you'd like some idea of my packing list the detail is in the Appendix but my aim was simple. I had to be as light as possible. Baggage would be two panniers at the rear, with a maximum load of five kilos in each. Basically, a spare pair of pants and a tool kit. Well, not quite, but you get the idea.

New cycles arrive at your local bike shop in cardboard boxes. I know, I was surprised too. So I reckoned that with a bit of research I could safely pack my bike into a cardboard box, and fly to southern Spain. There I would rebuild the bike on the roadside, placing all my packing material into the large waste containers you find there, jump on and ride.

Advice is available online about packing your bike for such a trip and I'd recommend you seek it out, but here is how I have done it twice now and will be how I plan such packing for future trips too. Some sites will recommend that you obtain your box from your local shop. You can, but bear in mind that they'll already have made one trip and may need some considerable strengthening before you can safely pack your own trusty steed. I buy new boxes that are basically too big - cut them down to size to be the largest I can get in the car - that's the first crucial measurement - and then strengthen the corners with yards and yards of tape emblazoned with the word 'Fragile'. I even write 'con cuidado, por favor' on the side when I've finished. Doffing my cap to the locals, of course. Ever the Englishman abroad.

Before   *Ready to go*

So here are my 'bike into the box' packing tips. My bike for these trips was a Specialised Allez 2010 with a triple set on the front.

Wheels.
Remove and take out the quick release skewers. Pop the skewers into a plastic bag and wrap with bubble wrap to be taped to the frame.Release a little air pressure out of tyres so that they are about half inflated. Apparently pressure at altitude forces tyres off the rim and letting the air out a little reduces this risk. Wrap the wheels in bubble wrap.
Frame.
Protect the frame with lengths of foam pipe cladding from your local DIY store. It's easy to cut to length and has a lengthwise split to allow easy fixing. Place a wooden block or similar between forks front and rear and fix in place with tape. This is to protect against a sideways knock that might force the forks together. It would have to be a good knock, but you are putting it on an aeroplane, so as much protection as you can is always the best bet.

Seat.
Lowered to the bottom. I haven't found it necessary to remove it, though some advice I found suggested that I should.
Pedals.
Removed and bubble wrapped. Tape them securely to the bike frame or the cranks.
Rear derailleur.
I found some advice that told me to remove this and tape it to the frame. However, I really didn't want to have to fix this tricky little blighter whilst crouching on the pavement, so my alternative approach was to protect it with a hard plastic food carton taped over it. It worked fine. You just need to be careful when sliding the wheels down the side of the box when packing though.
Chain.
I wrap this in pipe cladding too and tape it to the frame to stop it flopping around.
Pannier Rack
Don't forget that!
Handlebars.
Keep the cables connected but remove the bars and tuck them under the main frame. Again tape securely.
Tools.
Here's a crucial tip. Make sure that you pack the very tools that you used to strip down your bike. Getting to your destination to find that you've left your multi-tool on the kitchen table would not be a good start.
You're not going to get these through Security checks, so a small bag or two and taped securely to the bottom of the box is ample. When taping parts up make sure that there is no risk of anything coming loose. You really don't want loose bits of metal shaking in transit.
Swiss army knife.
This might be a bit 'Bear Grylls'[2] but I have one so I take it. I tape it to the underside of the box lid and then mark the spot with an 'X'. When I get to Spain that's my target area when beginning to unpack. Get in there first and the rest of the unpacking is simple.

I tape spare inner tubes and a few gels, because I like them, to the frame.

---

[2] Bear Grylls is an adventurer and tv presenter from Northern Ireland.

When it's all taped up, it is time to practice packing. There may be places where the frame and wheels press too firmly against the box sides. I reinforce these contact points with another layer of box cut to size. It can make packing a squeeze but its probably better not to have part of your bike hanging out of the sides when you get to the other end. Who knows what else you might lose? Cutting and reinforcing hand-holds is essential for ease of handling too.

Finally, I also pack a couple of bin liners just in case I need to scoop up my detritus into bags before disposing of it. And drop in a rag too. Putting your bike back together can be messy.

Fitness

I think that if you are reasonably fit then you can do something like cycling Spain coast to coast. And you will be able to tackle cycling at 3 or 4 thousand feet through the mountains if you just take your time. You're touring not racing.

Personally, I spent the winter months weight training and gym cycling until the weather was good enough for me to get out on the road. Then I made sure that I had a couple of spells where I would cycle for three days in a row working to a rough plan of Day 1 - 45 miles and the next 2 days at 50+ miles each. I'm assuming that you like cycling so the motivation won't be a problem. Just make sure you get some miles into your legs and you'll be fine. Oh, and make sure you like hills. It's no fun climbing the inevitable inclines if you have to keep getting off to push.

Route Planning

Quite simply, my plan was to fly to the south coast and ride to Santander for the ferry home. Route planning is time consuming but fun so be prepared to spend some time on it. There are lots of applications and tools to help you plan which give you estimated riding time, distance and elevation. I even checked out confusing junctions on Google Earth and made mental notes to look out for landmarks.

Also, many of the new motorways have been built alongside the old N roads, which are sometimes still used as access roads for service stations or by local farmers. They are less congested, often incredibly quiet, and more scenic. If you need to get somewhere quickly these options can be the best.

Finally, when booking your overnight accommodation it is best to make sure beforehand that you can keep your bike safe for the night. I've never had a problem, and the strangest security location I've left my bike is chained to a drainpipe on a service landing, but it's good to prepare your hosts too.

Plan your route - build in your rest days, if you are having any - upload to the cycle navigation tool of your choice (I used a Garmin Edge Touring). Your panniers are your carry on luggage. Your helmet, and I'm afraid, you must wear one in Spain, is your sunhat. You might get the occasional strange glance in the Boarding Lounge but hey, they might be just going for the beach, you're going on an adventure!

Cycling in Spain generally

In my experience the majority of Spanish roads have a cycle lane or wide shoulder where you can ride quite safely, and if you get tooted at from behind, it's always to let you know that there is a vehicle there, not the 'get-out-of-my-way' kind of toot. Spanish motorists are very tolerant of cyclists. I feel safer there than in England.

By law you must have a bell on your bike and not an alternative. It might not be sexy but it's not worth a fine. With regards to helmets, the law can be confusing. You don't need helmets in towns and cities (where the cars are!) but you must wear a helmet when you leave the conurbations. You don't have to wear a helmet going uphill or if it is extremely hot. It's all a bit variable. Personally, I've never come across a Spanish cyclist who is not wearing a helmet. I take my guidance from them.

Cyclists are allowed to ride anywhere except blue A and green E roads (motorways - check them on Google Earth!). Much the same as here, of course. However, some A roads can be minor roads too in some regions. But with infrastructure regeneration happening all the time you will occasionally find that an N road that you were happily cycling along has been improved and upgraded and is suddenly an A road.

It may even be an A road for a few miles and then revert to an N road. However, follow the signs, look for the prohibitive cycle signs and you should be fine. It just might mean that you have to make a detour. I know, it can be frustrating, particularly if you are riding into a major city. I write this in 2017. Check for any changes to road safety law online before you go.

Got your helmet and bell?

Let's go.

Ride 1
Malaga - Sevilla - Salamanca - Santander

		Miles
Day 1	Malaga to El Burgo	55
Day 2	El Burgo to Algodonales	45
Day 3	Algodonales to Sevilla	62
Day 4	Sevilla rest day	
Day 5	Sevilla to Monesterio	64
Day 6	Monesterio to Mérida	60
Day 7	Mérida rest day	
Day 8	Mérida to Cáceres	42
Day 9	Cáceres rest day	
Day 10	Cáceres to Plasencia	52
Day 11	Plasencia to Guijeulo	52
Day 12	Guijeulo to Salamanca	40
Day 13	Salamanca rest day	
Day 14	Salamanca to Tordesillas	53
Day 15	Tordesillas to Palencia	53
Day 16	Palencia to Aguilar de Campoo	61
Day 17	Aguilar to Comillas	60
Day 18	Comillas rest day	
Day 19	Comillas to Santander	30
		729

1. Malaga to Sevilla

Malaga's most famous son is probably Pablo Picasso. A man of passion and creativity and possibly the world's greatest artist. I guess that would be a point of debate. I had noticed a plaque honouring another famous son, Antonio Banderas, whilst out walking the shoreline one evening, bike rebuilt and ready to go. I can more relate to Antonio. I was broody and fidgety and impatient for the morning. I just needed to be on my way. The cultural hotspots of Malaga, celebrating their famous sons and daughters, would have to wait for another visit.

I knew that Day 1 would be a challenge. It was the first day on the bike for almost a week and my route planner showed that most of the second half of the ride would be into the mountains, so any normal assessment of timing would have to be extended. Plus I'm carrying 10 kilos on the back. Going into the mountains. Sounds romantic, doesn't it?

Before I left the UK a couple of friends had examined my plan, sucked

16

the cold winter air through their teeth and shaken their heads. Cycling Malaga to Sevilla in two days was a serious challenge, they suggested. One of them was Spanish and knew the road well. I bowed to their superior knowledge and split the trip into what I hoped would be three, manageable days.

And now the time had come. Malaga had entertained me long enough and it was time to head north. I was a little later setting off than planned so at just after 8.30 I set off into Malaga's rush hour.

Having walked the early stages of my route out of town the previous evening, I had picked up on the network of cycle routes which proved to be a great help. But what I hadn't bargained on, and who could, was an almost gale force headwind as soon as I hit the outskirts heading west. I was almost stopped in my tracks by gusts that took my breath away. Added to that, I was beginning to realise how heavy my bike actually was, now that I was carrying my worldly belongings in two bags strapped to the back.

It was grinding work and I quickly assessed that this was going to be a long ride. I conserved energy as best I could and gave myself all day to ride the distance and worked my way through it, eating and drinking constantly.

I had memorised by osmosis the route to El Burgo using my route planner and good old Google Earth. I knew that the ground would rise before the town of Coin and be relentlessly upward for the next twenty miles or more.

The head wind eventually dropped, thank goodness, which left me to climb the mountains. Just me, my bike, and the sun. I kept my head up, 'assumed the Froome'[3], and just got on with it. I am sure that I spent the next three hours in the lowest gear I have. I climbed and climbed and climbed some more. The route planner suggested a gentle gradient. Which, to begin with at least, it was. But a gentle gradient for thirty miles is a long sloooowwww climb.

I was headed into the Parque Natural Sierra de las Nieves - Sierra of the Snows - and the countryside was indeed beautiful in the late Spring sunshine. Olive groves by the score line the winding road up into the hills in this region. Every crested ridge offering views across the rolling landscape.

It was a hot lunchtime as I crawled into Alozaina, once voted Spain's Prettiest Village. An elderly man, passing the afternoon resting in the shade by a roundabout, kept himself awake by clapping his hands each time an element of traffic came by. Even I got a clap. A gesture of applause for getting this far up the mountain. We exchanged 'hola' - mine more breathless than his. I noticed that a police car, taking the bend slowly, received two claps. He was clearly respecting their authority.

But I didn't have time to stop and chat. I wasn't clear how far I still had to go and how long it would take me all uphill. I ground away. Aware of the sun but not feeling the heat necessarily. A breeze wafted by, more help in keeping me cool than a hindrance to progress.

Yunquera, my next landmark, was further than I thought. I knew that after this the road ramped up dramatically. Knowing this and having to address it after four and a half hours are two separate things. It ramped like hell. The surprising thing is that mentally you have no option but to go on. Stopping is not allowed. I kept throwing my inner chimp a well earned banana as each brow topped out to reveal the next one.

At last the top, for now, and I knew that from here I could just about freewheel into the tiny white-washed village of El Burgo, my bed for the night. As I rolled into El Burgo I felt elated. This had probably been the hardest ride I had ever completed. Pah, I spit on your English hills!

---

[3] Tour de France winner Chris Froome is noted for his seated climbing style with a high cadence.

I spent a very agreeable evening chatting over dinner with two doctors from Zurich. He, Swiss, a psychiatrist, and his wife, an Italian, paediatrician. They forsook their mother tongues and we had a very enjoyable evening, intrigued as they were, to discuss British politics and our myriad of opinions about Europe.

Checking out, I was getting used to cutting quite a dash in the colours of the day, los colores del dia. The proprietor of the small hotel told me that when he was young he was a cycling 'ganodoro' in the mountains. He was good, apparently. 'El rey de los montañas' , I say in my broken Spanish. He grins. Then he tells me that he had to stop due to a diagnosis of testicular cancer.

I respond with a sorrowful expression and take in his portly frame. Under there was once an athlete, I thought. It's true what they say about learning a language. You can understand more than you can actually say. I guess that's because as you build your vocabulary you can't pull the right words out of the drawer quick enough to actually say what you want to express.

El Burgo in the valley

The road out of El Burgo picked up where yesterday's efforts ended. More 12% gradient and a long slow grind to the top. There wasn't even any time for warm up! I was straight into it. But it was a beautiful morning. As I climbed higher and higher early morning mist in the valleys below began to melt away under the awakening rays of the morning sun. The light became clear and the air fresh. The silence of the mountain road proved the perfect backdrop to birdsong. Somewhere in the valley I heard a creaking tractor at its labours. Wild poppies flanked the roadside. Me, the road, and the mountain.

The scenery was stunning. I ached to stop and take pictures all the way up but I have learnt the hard way that taking pictures on the way down is far easier! Once you are into your climbing rhythm maintaining it is the trick.

As I climbed into the Sierra de las Nieves more cyclists swept past the tortoise calling a friendly 'buenos dias'. Saturday morning training rides - the same the world over.

Ultimately I peaked at the Puerto del Viento, at almost 1200 metres. Reaching the top and coasting down the other side was pure joy. I kept the speed down given that with two panniers on the back the bike might not always behave itself.

The whole area is just beautiful. For the first time in the ride I could sit up in the saddle and just enjoy. The road surfaces were gorgeous. Smooth, as they say, as babies bottoms. I rolled into Ronda ('Help, help

me Ronda') feeling pretty chuffed with myself. I didn't fall for Ronda's charms however. She's a fickle mistress, I hear.

The hard work in the mountains was done. Though there were some climbs still to do, I was able to enjoy some long speedy descents and take in the majesty of the Serrania De Ronda, an area of outstanding natural, jaw dropping, beauty.

It is funny how inanimate objects become your friends on solo trips like this. My bike will have ridden a few thousand miles with me by the time I complete this trip, all told. I might get him some orange walled tyres as a treat when this is over. And 'Mr.Garmin', never drinks, is cheap to keep, but a bit arrogant. Constantly insists that he is right. So, when I think he's right, I let him be right and when I think he's wrong, I tell him.

Rolling into Algodonales, he took me straight to the door of my bed for the night. A quaint, gorgeous little three roomed apartment which was part of a small terraced house in this old Spanish town in the hills. The heavy oak door had seen some years and if I lost my key I would be a few kilos lighter. Lock and key required some dexterity to work in partnership, but this was far more charming than a plastic-carded hotel room.

There is a natural feel to Spanish towns at siesta time. Whilst mid-afternoon is hot, it's not as hot as about an hour later when it is baking, and the only noise in town is the slurping of cerveza and the hum of gentle conversation. Such as it was in Algodonales. I bought an ice cream, a litre of water, and a cerveza and dealt with them in that order. I sat to watch the world go by - job done for the day.

I love live music but it is rare that I find myself arriving in a new town with the opportunity to indulge. With notable exceptions, I am either too early or too late for the show, the festival, the fiesta. I was forcing down my cerveza when I noticed a raised platform at the end of the square and I thought the pattern was repeating itself. Surprisingly, this was followed shortly afterward by the arrival of a municipal jeep to unload two speakers and a mixing desk. 'Wa-hey,' I thought, 'there's music tonight.' Heavily muscled grunts mumbled their 'Wun Too - Wun Too' to ensure that all the connections worked. But there was no sign of the band. Just a dais.

It is easy to forget in our stable western Europe that Spain's democracy is relatively new and only became a reality with the transition after Franco's death in 1975. The Spanish, therefore, cherish their vote and take their politics seriously. Of course, the passion of Spanish politics would come to our tv screens in 2017 with the Catalan crisis. That is a separate book in itself. For now, however, this was municipal election time on a hot early Saturday evening with a gathering crowd.

The wallpaper pop music was cut and the candidate took the stage. Pronouncements were met with neighbourly mutterings, applause here and there, and then, with a plea for their votes, he was gone to the next speaking engagement and everyone shuffled away. As political rallies go it was low key. In some countries the candidate wouldn't have bothered, preferring to focus on the numbers. But here, it seems, everyone deserves to hear from the man himself, and he should be congratulated for making the effort. The townsfolk will drink to that. Saturday night had begun.

5am Sunday. A rooster opens up a conversation with a braying donkey somewhere on the hillside and they're not shy about sharing their opinions. I mentally pushed "snooze" and rolled over. I planned to be up early for the longest ride of the trip so far - 70 miles. There was a sharp chill in the mountain air as I stepped out into the Algo morning. Sevilla sits in a geographical basin in the valley of the Guadalquivir River and benefits from a subtropical climate. In simple terms, it was going to get much hotter as the day wore on and so I intended to take my time. I resolved to stop at each petrol station and buy cold water. I'd failed to spot the benefits of insulated bottles before I left and in this sun the water quickly warms up. Regular drinking is critical but after a while the water is pretty tepid and its purely the need to hydrate that makes me drink it. My prep notes told me that I should check that I have everything I need at El Coronil, since after that point there are long stretches of 'notmuchness' in terms of fuelling stops for at least 30 miles or so.

As the sun rose into the day I eased along through waving masses of golden wheat fields and sunflowers breaking out their yellow fanned faces towards the sky leading me down to the delightful little town of El Coronil, a short hop off the main road at the end of an avenue of palm trees. Cars whip by the junction, heading for Ronda or Sevilla, not realising that down the hill is a little gem with a plaza just made for the Sunday papers, a coffee and conversation. Prayers said for the day, the gentry find a shady spot in the square to trade stories and diagnose creaking ailments. Bars are starting to open. People hail their friends for intense exchanges as if they haven't seen them for years.

I sipped coke, ate honey and tostados, and wiped dead flies from my shins, content as a group of mountain bikers came through on their club ride.

Back on the road in the hair dryer breeze, by 1.30 I had about 12 miles to go.

I messaged my hostess from a petrol station (cold water refill) to say that I would be early. No problem. I was whipping along. Oh, how pride comes before a fall.

My plan was to enter Sevilla by a route that would take me directly to my apartment and by some fortitude the slip road from the service station took me straight to the junction that I needed. I couldn't believe my luck. However, Mr.Garmin and I had an exchange of words. He kept telling me to u-turn and after a couple of these false starts I realised that I was going around in circles. But I was only 5 miles from Sevilla. What could go wrong?

To cycle into Sevilla you need to have your route planned meticulously, it seems. Take this from someone who has now experienced it. Cycles are banned from the major A roads into the city even though you've been on the same road for the last 50 miles.

So it was that I found myself at a roundabout facing A roads to Malaga, Jerez and Sevilla and the only other option, somewhere called "San Pedro", notified by a rough hand painted sign. "San Pedro" it is then.

I began to feel a little uneasy as I bounced along a moon-cratered dirt track between slatted sheds and corrugated shacks, junked cars, machinery and broken glass. I could hear raucous voices and laughter from the 'chabolistas', shanty-town dwellers, but saw no-one and I hoped that I wasn't going to attract any attention. I felt that this was probably the last place I should be right now. A guard dog thought that I was sport and gave chase, yapping alarm until I managed to outrun him. What am I doing here?

I stumbled out onto a minor road unscathed and thankful but my bike was limping. Impossible to dodge everything as fast as I could, I'd whacked the rim of a hole resulting in a hole in my tyre.

By now it was 35 degrees and I'm by the roadside repairing my tyre, getting hotter, hungry and tired. I needed to drink, but my water tasted like I'd done my washing in it. During the next 20 minutes I was passed by half a dozen different vehicles of some sort. One asked if I would like a lift in his truck, with the bike in the back, and 3 more stopped to see if I was okay. I remembered a conversation with my Spanish friend before I left home. I'd said I was worried about mechanical failures on the road. "Don't worry," she said, "there'll always be someone to help you." And so it seemed.

Sunday siesta Sevilla. Six lane highways and hardly a car in sight. It had taken me two and half hours to work out the last 12 miles. My hostess, Barbara, greeted me with a smile and handshake. She didn't seem to mind my oily fingers. She was a cyclist too and we joked that if you get a puncture it is usually the back wheel - the dirty one. First things first, she poured me ice cold water from the fridge and I drank like a man who'd just crawled through a desert. We went through the practiced routine with me very conscious of my grubby state. It had indeed been a long hot ride. I was in Sevilla at last. I just love siestas.

2. Sevilla to Mérida

Sevilla is a 2,000 year old city of some grandeur, reflecting in its architecture and atmosphere, the colourful history of Spain. I had arrived in mid-May and already the streets were awash with visitors seeking out the beautiful cathedral, the stunning Plaza de España and the amazing Metropol Parasol - Las Setas, the mushrooms, as the locals call it. With characteristic tardiness, I had missed the Flamenco festival. It would have to be the side street flamenco bars that would satisfy this particular itch.

24

I had planned a single rest day here to take the opportunity to explore, so there was no time to waste queueing at the major attractions.I wandered the warren of old streets, the comfortable green squares and gardens and the innumerable bars, soaking up the atmosphere of one of the world's oldest cities.

A group of teenagers kicked a ball around underneath the Metropol Parasol. Behind them, weeds grew from the windowsills of a fading grandee of Sevillian architecture. I wondered if they saw its beauty or do locals only see an eye sore. Possibly.

Daytime heat barely gave way to evening heat. Flamenco has an unrivalled passion and drama, 'el duerte', as the Spanish would say. As my explorations for the day came to an end the night was still definitely young.

Flamenco has to be experienced. It is the live environment that drives this music forward and into your heart and soul. I have been told that there is a difference between 'tourist' flamenco and the real gypsy deal which you won't get to see without some guidance from a chaperone. It's not something you stumble across.

You can't miss what you never had and tonight the show is a delight.

Sparks flew from snapping heels to the call of a mournful tenor. The guitar, once delicate, now rasps a thunderous beat. I sauntered home with the mood of someone having to leave the party early.

Despite my best efforts, I only managed about 4 hours sleep. Nevertheless, I felt lively enough as I woke. Luckily leaving Sevilla was much easier than getting in. The sun rising, the warmth slowly building, commuter journeys were in full flow. A network of cycle paths led me through a section of the abandoned Expo '92 site with its futuristic gestures and empty shell buildings. It was wonderfully eerie,

just waiting to be explored. Sadly, today there would be no time. An exploration of the site would have to be one of those joys for another day. I crossed a car park and ducked through a passage running under the road into the suburbs.

You can plan rides around your home town and generally speaking you know what you are going to get. The delight of attempting something like this though is that every day, every corner, offers up opportunity. Oddly, for a week-day morning, I rounded an innocent looking corner in an innocent enough street to find myself involved in a parade, tucked in between horse drawn carriages, driven by men in pressed green jackets, wide brimmed Sevillano hats, and ladies resplendent in wedding cake dresses with red poppy trims and seductive fans. Occasionally a trumpet blew. There I was - my own float at the carnival - solo cyclist. I was as bemused as the onlookers. I trailed behind a horse drawn buggy. Two gentlemen of this parish having a good old chin wag.

Fortunately the carnival came to a sudden halt at a junction, presumably whilst they could spot a break in the traffic to bring it all to a stop. A member of the Guardia Civil spotted me as I looked for a way out and then came to my rescue by holding everyone up, carnival and traffic, and waving me through. I was, after all, in the way, I guess. I nodded my "grazias" to him and sped on leaving the carnival to wander on its way.

Carnival Parade? Tuesday?   Ask no questions. This is the wonder of living for the moment in the kaleidoscope of Spain.

There is a road somewhere in Scotland which is an optical illusion. By sight, you seem to be travelling uphill, but in actuality you are travelling downhill. The technical term for this illusion is 'an electric bray' . Little did

I know that I was to experience this phenomenon today, except in reverse. I thought I was going downhill when it felt like up. The Ruta de la Plata, or Road of Boredom, extends from Sevilla to Astorgo and was built by the Romans. Fortunately it has been resurfaced since then, but they clearly didn't feel the need to stop and chat. The number of towns along the route are few, and in between them, not much else. Picture a snooker table. Raise one end by about 6 inches, just enough to create a long steady incline, and place a snail at the low end. When said snail has reached 2/3 of the way up, say, about the Pink spot, blow a hairdryer into his face to slow him further. That is pretty much what the ride felt like. Looking back on the day now, I don't think I was fuelled enough for miles 10 to 20. Early in the ride I know, but after only about 4 hours sleep, early enough. By lunch time I was well behind the pace and the Road of Boredom just went on and on ...

The Ruta de la Plata was first used as a commercial route. The name is derived from the Arabic meaning for 'cobbled way' although to the Romans, Ruta de la Plata means 'silver route/road' ....until it was renamed by a tired grumpy tourist as the Route of Boredom.

I needed desperately to get my engine going. No matter how I tried, the old legs were misfiring. I stopped at every (!) petrol station and bought fuel and sugary drinks. Fuel being food. Even one ham and cheese sandwich whose use by date was the 1st June - two weeks hence. How many preservatives were in that?!

Eventually the food fuel kicked in and after lunch I was able to pick up the pedal rate a little, inspired by seeing Monesterio appear on road signs. Around 4.00 pm, much later than planned, I passed a sign saying 'Monesterio 10'. I was almost there. I threw my inner chimp another banana and pushed on.

The last 5k was the most evil climb for the end of a ride along the most boring road on the hottest day. I pulled into my Truck Stop watering hole for the night and put the whole day down to knowing that it was a ride that had to be done. It had taken me 8 hours to do 65 miles. I was utterly exhausted.

Welcome to Extramadura. There isn't much of a tourist trade around these parts, at least not until Mérida. Monesterio is on the route to somewhere else. Santiago de Compostela, for instance. So you are not going to find much English spoken and the local dialect comes at you with the mercy of a Gatling Gun. My 'Estudio Español, pero no entiendo rapido' usually buys me a second shot at 90% velocity. And then with a few waves and nods we will arrive at a consensus of understanding. My Spanish is unashamedly, and for obvious reasons, touristic. But the more I am being immersed in the language with no other options, the more I am enjoying speaking Spanish and being understood.

Bike stowed away safely and myself cleaned up for the evening, I sat in the hotel reception area to catch up on the day's news and gulped on my first cold beer. I was tired and grateful but something wasn't quite right. My beer smelled odd and I wasn't sure that I could even drink it. I felt the urge to bring this to the attention of the barman who sniffed it in wonder, looked at me quizzically, said that it smelled of beer, poured it away and gave me another. After a few more swigs and sniffs, I was forced to acknowledge that he was right - it smelled of beer. All this in Spanish. He might think that I'm a prat (un pratto) but at least I get points for making the effort and it's amazing what you can drink when you need one.

I feasted like a ravenous beast on steak and chips, knowing that my exhaustion was down to lack of food and sleep, and then hit the sack very early, and to my joy, despite the companionship of a mosquito on a scooter, I slept like a baby.

Up with the morning chill and on the road, trees give way to barrenness for a while as I ride high across the plains. My exhaustion over, I felt great. Today was a new day.

This is a high flat land with an accompanying breeze and even though I was riding into a headwind for most of the day I was able to make good time.

The landscape offers thousands upon thousands of vines and olive trees. Stretching for miles. Planted in neat rows an ancient tractor width apart. A weary car, parked under a tree, alerts the passerby to a dusty farmer somewhere up with the lark, dragging dead branches, vine stocks and weeds into heaps for burning. The task of tending these vines and trees must be overwhelming but where would we be without them?

There is livestock here too. You can't see it this early in the day but the unmistakable odour wafts on the wind.

The towns I ride through seem livelier than the ones south of Monesterio. Once in a while I find myself on a road which is arrow straight as far as the eye can see, the panoramic vista studded with bodegas. Oh, if only I could stop and sample. But no, I must be disciplined.

Just as the day's siesta is kicking in, I pick my way down into Mérida through a lovely park where children are laughing and playing in the sun, entering the city as the Arabs had done centuries ago - over the bridge that the Romans built.

Mérida is the capital of the region. Named by the Arabs when they overthrew the Romans in 713 AD but it is the Romans who have left their mark here. The new Muslim rulers kept the Roman buildings and used them as their seat of authority.

As I go through my routine, emptying water into plant containers by the

roadside, finding my passport amongst my bags of jelly babies, loosening my helmet and freeing my hair, prima donna style, the concierge greets me with a smile and wheels my bike into the hotel for me. The first time, and probably the only time, the bike gets there before I do.

Wandering Mérida is a feast of surprises. A seemingly unremarkable row of shops is suddenly lifted by your stumbling upon an ancient Roman artefact, an arch, or the columned frontage of some ministerial building. Modern Mérida has been built around the old in such a way as to preserve and honour its heritage. The contrast is startling and enriching. You almost feel

30

llke breaking into applause. It would have been so easy to tear it down and build over it.

Anyone visiting Mérida should head for the Amphitheatre and gardens, a stunningly preserved Roman complex of atmosphere and drama where gladiator reputations were won and lost, hierarchy entertained, and plots hatched amongst the gardens. I strolled freely with the ghosts of toga clad governors and laurel wreathed heroes. It just takes a little imagination and you're there.

3. Mérida to Cáceres

I enjoyed Mérida and in a way was sorry to leave. For the last three days I have been following, well, the tarmac bits anyway, the south to north route of the Camino de Santiago. That well known route of pilgrimage for those desperate to see one of the world's biggest incense

burners, the Botafumeiro - big smoke blower - as well the formidable cathedral of St. James itself. Not to mention the forgiveness of sins. Blue shell waymarkers spot the road north and there is a sense of following something steeped in historic significance, almost as if the journey itself is as important as the destination. Very zen indeed.

I'm not a particularly religious person but each to his own, as they say. Even then, having said that, you cannot help but be moved by the emotional pull of following this route. The early stages of my morning ride out of Mérida took me through a nature reserve, on a road worn ragged by the fall of the steps of thousands of penitent feet. I was keen not to repeat my puncture experience arriving into Sevilla a few days ago and so wandered across the road for the smoothest line.

Eventually back on smooth tarmac, I encountered for the first time pilgrims following the Camino. Pilgrims are identifiable by the wearing of shells somewhere upon their person and often by their joyous enquiry as you approach them. These two chaps were sitting by the roadside taking a break, their bikes laden like mechanical donkeys. I suspect they were rather pushing them than riding them. Two chaps, weary travellers both, and both looked like apostles, at least all the pictures I've ever seen of apostles - long beard and needing a good wash.

As I approached they called to me, 'Baa Santiago?'

'No,' I replied, 'Cáceres y ultima Santander'. This mini-synopsis of my coast to coast was met with a non-plussed grunt. Perhaps the people of Santander are going straight to Hell. If so, I think they should be told.

Oh well, not all sinners can be saved, and I reflect that they'll probably reach Santiago by August.

Despite a headwind I reached Cáceres and my apartment in the old town in good time, fortified as I was, by a lunch of cheese sandwich, banana, and an ice cream from a roadside petrol station. My apartment is located on a steep narrow street typical of these old towns. There are small cars parked, tucked into corners, slotted in like stumps in a wicket, but I'm glad I'm cycling. I would never try to get a car in here.

Rooftops of the beautiful old town of Cáceres

Cáceres is the second largest town in Extramadura and has apparently taken the brunt of the downturn in the Spanish economy after the financial crash, since its main economic driver was, or is, the construction industry. However, once you have worked your way through the trappings of any modern city, high rise blocks, shopping and industrial estates, the centre of the old town is a world heritage site and a kernel of culture. I should mention that I am typically late for the WOMAD Cáceres.

Whenever I visit Spain I am enthralled by the mix, almost the continuation of the rivalry, between Christian and Islamic influences in architecture and history. The bloody conflicts of the time have left us with a legacy of cross-cultural art that must surely be celebrated, though I know that in some circles the conflicts of the past remain a preoccupation of the present. The Alhambra in Granada and the Mosque/ Cathedral in Cordoba are excellent examples of what has been preserved. There are few Moorish examples remaining in Cáceres since rival factions between the 12th and 14th centuries did their worst, but they are here, visible in the brickwork of alleyways and houses.

4. Cáceres to Salamanca

Storks, sitting atop their nests, themselves atop the pinnacles of the church of Santiago in Cáceres, threw back their heads and clacked in the early morning. There seemed some serendipity to it all as I too clacked my way across cobbled streets in my cycling shoes. We were chilled, storks and I, but I suspect that they are tougher. I'm thankful that I packed arm warmers for these occasions. The storks were higher than me, of course, they could have been shivering. The deep narrow streets of Cáceres gave me shelter until I hit the outskirts heading north.

33

Eventually free of empty industrial units, I felt the full force of the north-easterly wind that was to blow for the rest of the day.

I had wondered if a headwind, sweeping down from the the Bay of Biscay, would be a feature of riding north from this point. Fortunately, my training at home had been on many a blustery day, as Pooh would say. I spent much of the first two hours trying to avoid the effects of such a blast. Frequently crouching down onto the "drops" to reduce wind resistance and chill. By the time I had reached the top of the steep climb halfway through the ride, I had my first injury of the journey so far - runners nipples. Oooohh. I pulled over and reached into my bag for my butt cream, guessing that I might have to start applying to my moobs in future.

This was to be a 55 mile ride with only two towns along the road between Cáceres and Plasencia, my next stop. But the landscape was changing as I approached the hills in the distance. Everything becoming much greener.

I had been looking forward to riding by the huge Embalse de Jose Maria Oriol, a lake served primarily by the Rio Tajo. This was one of the creations resulting from the building of the Alcantara Dam some several miles further west. The gulleys along the lake gave me respite from the wind and it was a delight to see the deep blue of the water. The Rio Tajo, however, is a hefty river and hefty rivers need bridges …

The lakeside road meandered for miles and there was much leaning into corners, bending of knee and snapping of throttle wrist as leather clad warriors navigated the 'curvas peligrosas'. They were clearly having noisy fun. No-one was waving them down, the roads were clear and even I could appreciate the bikers dream.

It was along this stretch that I came across more pilgrims. Serious walkers all, carrying long wooden sticks, wearing shorts that gave way

to weathered skin. This is a long way on a bike. To walk it calls for some serious commitment, and I assume, a strong faith. Good luck to them. I'm sure that they have lots of thinking time.

Plasencia is not as charming as Cáceres and what's more, since it is Sunday siesta time, it is not only closed, but staying closed until tomorrow. It does, however, have its historical buildings as a result of being on the Ruta de la Plata for centuries and the significance that all that brought. Tonight I shall be staying in the parador here. A beautiful ancient building with atmosphere to spare, and it would seem, a group of German cyclists who enlivened Checking-In by laughing and joking at each others expense.

Directed to my room, I squeezed into the tiny lift with another lycra clad specimen, for specimens in a jar is more or less what we looked like. In the uncomfortable silence surrounded by mirrors we tried vainly not to look ridiculous, pulling in our paunches as best we could. I checked for CCTV and dared to break the silence. It was only getting worse. Better to divert attention. It transpired that my fellow cyclist was one of a group of businessmen having a ball cycling from one parador drinking opportunity to the next, aided by a support car, which scooped them up if they became too tired. As an alternative to the golfing holiday, I thought, it had to be more fun.

The parador is a 15th century monastery of Santo Domingo. I pulled the bell rope above my bed hoping for room service, but with a quarter of a mile of rope to twitch not a sound was heard downstairs. No-one came to disturb the night. I suspect that in the old days they probably sent a runner with guest instructions.

As the birds sang and the cowbell clanged I pulled off my nightshirt and night cap, reached for my morning flagon of ale and turned on the tv. From the news reports covering the recent elections it was clear that Spain had swung to the Left. Perhaps there had been a new Socialist revolution and I would have to get my own breakfast.The world is forever changing.

And talking of flagons, I tried a white wine last night, from this region, and made from the Pardina grape. I swirled like the gourmand that I am.

My tasting notes are;

Aromatic bouquet
Glossy finish
Pale golden in colour
A hint of sweetness though not too much

Interesting summer plonk

Plonk points: 80/100.

With nipples greased, and everything else, I was ready for the road. It was a beautiful morning. The sun was warming up quickly and there's no wind. Joy.

The hills in the distance beckoned and whilst that means more climbing it does also mean trees and views to appreciate. The landscape was going to change once more. I passed several large derelict buildings on the way. Not worthy of much note perhaps but I do love to reflect on the stories those walls could tell.Their inhabitants long gone in the name of progress or simply the passing of time.

Many of the towns that I pass through boast cafés, bars and restaurants but I think I am too early in what might present itself as a tourist season, since many remain closed. Given that it is nearly the end of May, I'm not sure when their 'season' starts and this leaves me dependent upon the Great god, Repsol, bringer of food and drink, to keep me rolling down the road.

I take my lunch on the crumbling steps of the old church at Baños de Monte Mayor, which stares down at the traveller as he passes below. Taking the sun with my ham and cheese croissant I pondered the impact and passions aroused by the Christian faith in Spain.

I had rested the night in a convent, photographed and wandered ancient medieval churches, wondering at their artwork, overheard the strains of choral practice through an open window in Sevilla, and here I was, eating lunch on the steps of another, perhaps forgotten, pillar of faith. Spain and the Catholic Church have existed hand in glove since the 15th century, except for a couple of short notable periods when republican tendencies strained at the authority of the Church. The outcome of Spain's Civil War saw Franco's rule cement the Church at the heart of life in Spain once again. However, with the death of Franco and the transition to democracy the State declares itself neutral in religious affairs. This secularism may curb church influence, but a report of 2010 still shows 76% of Spaniards declaring themselves to be Catholic, if not all church-goers.

I wondered if Spain would go the way of the UK and become a more secular society as younger generations grow up steeped in cynicism and instant messaging. Such is how my mind wanders.

I was also intrigued by the name of the town. Baños? Half way up a hill? Rambling through the town it became quite clear that there is a tourist market here. Souvenir shops abound building business on the back of the Roman Baths that are situated in the centre of town.I was happy to climb out of Baños de Monte Mayor. Thick trees rich in greenery camouflaged the birdsong. What I didn't realise at the time was that this was the start of 3 hours of climbing. On and up, before I would reach Guijuelo for respite.

Baños de Monte Mayor from the hill

Guijuelo is a small industrial town with a population of 6000 and my instincts as I explored a little were that it reminded me of many a small working class town back home. The main road runs right through the middle and on either side of it appear valiant attempts to make a living by serving the community.

Incomes may have dropped since the boom years and times may be harder, but throughout this trip, I have found the Spanish people to be nothing but helpful, kind and patient with my broken Spanish language. Desperate for a beer (I'd inadvertently booked a barless hotel) I wandered towards the Main Square to find the only bar open, The Sheriff. Ordering my cerveza and handing over my €2 coin the Señora checked her till. She didn't have a 10 cent piece for my change so gave me my money back, and despite my protestations, insisted that I have a free beer. A simple gesture that lit up my day after a long grinding climb and a warming example of the kindness of one stranger to another. It was cool and tasted delicious though as refreshing as it was I thought it imprudent to ask for another.

The following morning I rise to something of a shock to the system. I had crossed some invisible boundary line between south and north that would lay out the make up of the days for the rest of the ride. I entertained myself by making up my own weather forecast. BBC plum voice: ' Here is the cycling forecast for northern Spain. Today, 26th May 2015. Extramadura. East by North Easterly. Blustery. Gustery.' Today I finally cracked out my wind cheater. Boy, was it cold? Even though the sun was up its impact was absent. My wind jacket is of the 'boil in the bag' variety. Light as it is and effective against the wind, there is little ventilation, leaving you to accumulate body moisture to point of feeling that you have created your own rain shower. I slowly get wetter and wetter on the inside. All I would need to do to dry out later was to find a windless spot in the sun and slowly turn myself, rotisserie style, well basted. Fortunately today was to be a short ride, 33 miles or so, but demanding in the strongest wind yet.

I stopped into a roadside Meson Ibérico for refreshments and sampled one of her Ladyship's tapas which was so tasty it caused me to comment on the quality of her cooking. Which, thankfully, she took in the spirit in which it was intended and not as a proposal of marriage.Though if she cooks like that...I arrived in Salamanca just after 2pm. My hotel is part of the Plaza Mayor, an economy part, I might add, so that I have the tiniest room they have. After squeezing my bike into the lift, it is now safely chained to a sewage pipe on an outside service terrace only accessed by the staff.

But who comes to a town like this and stays in their room? Old Salamanca has been a UNESCO World Heritage site since 1988 and one of the most important university cities in the western world for centuries. Today, a fifth of its population are students. Wandering the old town you can easily see why this is a top destination for students from around the world. The streets ooze charm and history and the sandstone buildings glow in the sunshine.

The Plaza Major is in constant use throughout the day as a thoroughfare and as a place to meet and socialise or, as I witnessed on several occasions, just treating the space as a concrete beach and laying out in the sun. I spent a lot of time here just watching people transition from one side of the square to the other. Salamancans going about their business.

'I just love Salamanca,' exclaimed Julie, an American student from San Diego,'I've been here about 9 months and it's just fantastic. I love it,' she giggled. Unfortunately, this wasn't an exclusive interview. Julie was telling her friend just off the plane... and the rest of the restaurant. Okay, I forgive her. I'd fall in love with it too.

I had decided, when planning the trip, that Salamanca was going to be the stop where I reviewed everything for the final week. Baggage, planning, riding experiences and so on.

It had become clear as my ride brought me further north that I hadn't planned, for instance, for the temperature drop in the mornings. I was

under-dressed for the chilly morning starts. What was needed were more base layers. Likewise, washing every evening was fine in the south, where the air temperature was high all day and you could rely upon your smalls being dry by the morning. Further north, everything begins to get a bit chillier. In fact, it is more like England on a summer's day than Spain basking in the glory of a heatwave.

Another factor to account for was the headwind. I had in mind that there might be one, but I hadn't factored in its dilatory effect on speeds and mileage. I had been training in winds in England during the spring and was used to it, but the impact feels somewhat greater when you are dragging your belongings with you!

Therefore, with all this in mind, baggage was rationalised and anything unlikely to be needed or not used so far was dumped to create room for the final essentials.

Thus it was that I bought two more base layers in Salamanca, two more t-shirts to ease the pressure on washing, and rationalised my mileage for the next two days.

I had given myself the task of covering the next 110 miles or so in two chunks, 80 today then 30 or 40 tomorrow. I considered that if the headwind was as strong as it was reaching Salamanca, then an 80 mile ride is likely to leave me drained and dishevelled. So my plans changed to break up the ride into 53 today and the balance tomorrow. So, I will be aiming for Tordesillas.

It turned out to be a lovely ride out of Salamanca, even though the traffic was fast and furious, probably because the roads are generally dead straight. There was no wind after all. Warm sun, and rolling agricultural landscape. Salamanca really is a jewel. If you've been there you know that, if you haven't, put it on your list.

5. Salamanca to Comillas

The sun shone and the fields rolled by. I shed my extra layers by 11.00am and pushed on. One of the things I have learnt in reviewing the last stages is that, even though I think I can do the miles, it really isn't worth pushing on so much that I miss the experience. I remind myself to take the time to stop and smell the roses, or the poppies, as they say.

In that context, I have grown to appreciate the roadside. This may sound very strange, but frequently I find myself riding by wild blue cornflowers, mingled with a riot of poppies, against a backdrop of golden wheat. It is, I tell you, quite beautiful.

The roads are often so quiet that birdsong is the only accompaniment to the solitary cyclist. I came across two snakes and a large lizard trusting to the barren road. The larger snake unfortunately had recently had his trust misplaced and the smaller one almost went the same way, camouflaged as he was to the approaching cyclist, against the road surface. The lizard, too quick for anyone.

Aleajos was today's planned lunch stop. I rolled into town, Clint Eastwood style, examined as I sauntered by, by local gentry kicking back into the early afternoon. Stranger in town. (Whistles.) And it is market day.

I cause more attention as I wheel my bike between the stalls and head for the Pan Van. The market itself looks much like you would experience in England, everyday essentials and a call to have your dog vaccinated against rabies. A market trader spots me and wanders over. It is about 28 degrees and he is wearing a heavy coat. He asks if I am English (how could he tell?) and says that he understands a little English. In response to his enquiry about my Spanish I confirm 'a little'. It seems that touring on his motorbike is his thing, so I tell him that I am riding from Malaga to Santander. He compliments me and says that I must be strong. I don't know about that, but I smile and thank him anyway.

Then he questions me on the preparation of my bike, trying with this thumb to create some impression in the rock hard surface of my rear tyre. He repeats the question and tries to create a dent again, as if to query the simple practical mechanics of pedalling from one town to another. Meanwhile, I can't seem to pull the necessary Spanish vocabulary from my mental drawer. Maybe the words I need are not there anyway. I hadn't thought that the Spanish for 'to blow up' was a verb I would need. At least not unless it was in conjunction with 'I wish to speak to the British Embassy'.

He wished me a 'bien viaje' and I thanked him. He had a stall to attend to and he'd worked out for himself that I had inflated my tyres to a rock hard standard.

I bought an empanada from the Pan Man and what a fine empanada it was indeed. Family sized, and laid out flat on a piece of cardboard box, it provided lunch for the following day too.

Whilst Baños de Monte Mayor may have been a bit of a mystery, in the beginning at least, Siete Iglesias (seven churches) is pretty obvious. But as I approached the next village I could only see one from the road and I couldn't be bothered to find the other six.

And with that Tordesillas came up quicker than I expected. It had been a good ride and I had completed 53 miles in 4 and a half hours.

43

Tordesillas is famous for its annual Toro de la Vega festival, which involves a bull being chased by townsfolk to the meadow by the river. The event culminates in the eventual slaughter of the main protagonist.The festival has been celebrated for the last 500 years and depictions of the "spectacle" decorate the bull statue which stands at the entrance to the town. At the time of my ride, this was still an annual event eliciting some outrage amongst those who see the traditional event as a barbaric practice. Which, to a non-Spaniard at least, it probably is. However, as a visitor to the country, I'm not about to press my value system on a people who have done me no harm and rather, have treated me with nothing but kindness.

That said, at the time of writing, things have changed. In May 2016 the Regional Government passed a decree prohibiting the slaughter of the bull in public.Those who defended the festival were not happy and even today tension remains between those who called for an end to the festival and those who campaign to retain it with its attendant slaughter. Consequently, every September the Toro de la Vega continues in Tordesillas but the death of the bull, having been chased and taunted, takes place behind closed doors. This is Spain, in all its complexities and traditions.

And so onwards. The second leg of my rescheduling should see me ride over 50 miles again. It is a beautiful morning, with little or no breeze to speak of, and I roll through endless fields of farmland.

The route I take is a deviation from the N roads, which shadow the main motorways, so it is some relief from the drone that has accompanied some stretches during the last few days. I intended to get to Valladolid before lunchtime and then navigate my way to the start of my preplanned Valladolid to Palencia ride. That should leave me with about 35 miles to do after noon. I always spend half an hour each evening just getting the following day's ride in my head. I knew that I shouldn't go near Valladolid centre and that I could scoot around, approaching from the west, to pick up my route North, if I just kept my wits about me. Sure enough, chuffed as I was, I did the scooting, and was heading north out of Val by 11.45 am.

The villages came quickly and it was a real motivator to knock them off one by one. I had energy in the bank and so I made a deal with myself. The first town to be able to sell me a Coke (other fizzy drinks are available), without me deviating from my route, becomes my lunch stop. Wow, did they let me down?!

Eventually, conscious of the passing of time between eating, hunger won, and I pulled into Cigales looking forward to parking my rear and enjoying my empanada Part Dos. I was impressed by Cigales as I rode in. It seemed to be spotless, with modern housing, cheek by jowl with more traditional elements, in streets exuding a certain charm.

I found myself a drink and pastry at a corner shop, much to the amusement of the shopkeeper and her customer, whose gossipy conversation I was clearly interrupting with my strange appearance. I rested in the shade in the market square to tuck in and watched the world go by. Just an ordinary town with its townsfolk living an ordinary day I did wonder why they had decided to put a tobacco kiosk adjacent to the church. Was Mass so demanding as to require a smoke to calm your nerves?

The Main Square in Cigales.....this view on my right

.....and this view on my left

Cigales was denominated as a wine region in 1991. Its main virtue being that traditional methods are still very much to the fore around these parts. The climate is harsh with low rainfall but that still hasn't triggered the use of modern chemicals and fertilisers in the viniculture. Sadly, cycling and wine don't mix. Maybe next time.

I was contented with the morning's work, my spirits only dampening a little as I watched the once lifeless Spanish flag flutter in what I knew was a lifting breeze. You may have noted my comments so far about the occasional headwind. The impact is intensified by that fact that there really is nowhere to hide. Many roads are dead straight for very long stretches ensuring that shelter, even briefly, is a rare thing indeed.

This area is known as the Tierra de Campos, a wide vast agricultural plain, with dry, fertile clay soil and adapted farming methods giving the landscape a patchwork quilt appearance.

And the wind blew gusterly blusterly.

As luck would have it, I pulled out in front of a tractor hauling a loaded hay cart. He was about 100 yards behind and we both seemed to be doing the same speed. Aha, I thought. My peloton. I stopped to let him overtake me so that I could ride right behind him, hidden from the wind and hidden from view, with the smell of fresh cut hay drifting over me. I managed this for a few miles before he turned off but the "in flight" rest was welcome.

Palencia was quiet and, of course, hot, when I arrived. It seemed to offer little by way of charm as, gently perspiring yet wind chilled, I pushed my heavy load through the tightly woven streets to my resting place. All I could see were closed shops, streets and streets of them. Proper exploration would have to wait.

The ferry back to the UK sails twice a week. I knew I wouldn't make the Sunday sail, therefore Wednesday it is, and so Palencia was set to be another rest over town.

Like many Spanish towns on this trip, medieval churches stand as stubborn reminders of a glorious past, as modernity, with its mercurial spread, shuns its foundations and moves on around them. I found the cathedral and, failing to spot the sign that said the entrance was for

worshippers only, I found myself in a secluded corner of the vast building listening to some lovely Latin anthem and hoping that my ungodly dress wouldn't attract attention. There was a service in full flow.

Realising my error, after a short while, I crept out, found the tourists entrance, and paid the cathedral the respect it deserved.

Skulking out and then back in again seemed a fateful way for me to stumble, into the bronze cast, conical hatted penitents outside the Church of San Pablo. It is always an arresting image, though our first thought these days seems always to be of the poisonous KKK. The wearing of conical hats, or capirotes, is a centuries old Spanish tradition denoting Christian brotherhoods

47

of various persuasions.

The capirotes themselves vary in colour as identifiers and are worn by those serving penance for their sins, with the face covering veil to hide their shame. Nowadays, the wearing of the capirote is reserved for festivals and Holy Week, or Semana Santa, but still it is difficult to shake off their modern sinister equivalent.

The Church might think it rules the roost but it's the Plaza Mayor where the action happens. Having not had the opportunity to make this a musical experience, it was ironic that Palencia came up with the goods. With a beer in hand, I pondered the stage in front of the Town Hall, amused by the antics of sound men and serious roadies whose stern expressions as they went about their jobs were an amusing backdrop to testing the efficacy of a plug.

Square-side bars grew noisy as the early afternoon loomed and the friendly familiar gatherings sprang up all around me. If there is one thing the Spanish like to do, it is talk. The community spirit was alive and well.

The stage, it seems, was set for a trio. The soundcheck piqued my interest, so I resolved to stick around. After all, despite my earlier comment, live music was becoming a feature of the trip. When the band eventually appeared at about 2.00pm, the sun and the beer was kicking in and the crowd were ready to dance. What transpired was a sort of Spanish Buzzcocks[4].

I shuffled around to the merchandise stall, inquisitively searching out CDs, and found that the group was called Novedades Carminha. Surely did they rock a very appreciative crowd with some energetic and catchy riffs. I stayed to the end. Palencia had come good.

Leaving town on a Sunday morning was generally a quiet affair, except for the occasional parishioner who appeared to be late for church. I'd had an appropriately light dinner and a good night's sleep the previous evening, despite the 2am crazies who I think were eventually expelled from the hotel. Maybe it was the band being rock and roll.

Utilising my extensive meteorological knowledge of how wind forms - land heats up, heats up air, hot air rises, cold air moves in to replace hot air = wind - I banked on the premise that with a good start I could probably get 50 miles done by 1.00 pm, which would leave the remainder of the ride to do into the wind, if my previous experiences were anything to go by.

My plan looked like it might work. There wasn't so much as a whisper in the air. I cracked on. By 1.00 pm I had completed 47 miles and that was good enough for me.

---

4 The Buzzcocks were a punk rock group, formed in the UK, in 1976.

For the first time on my journey I found myself travelling along by a canal, the Canal de Castilla. The canal was built in the late 18th and early 19th centuries to facilitate the transportation of wheat. When the railroads came, all that changed and it is now used as the spine of an elaborate irrigation system.

The presence of water was a pleasant addition though the presence of midges could have been improved by their being somewhere else! I was cycling along happily wondering what the tickling was on my face and then realised that I was blasting through clouds of midges at head height.

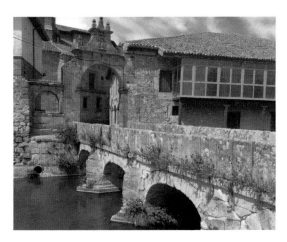

Aguilar de Campoo sits on the Rio Pisuerga, which is 'locked' in the town itself and rests in the shadow of the Aguilon rock, upon which stands the remains of a 12th century fort. The church of San Miguel stands at the end of an arcaded rectangular plaza but is closed when I arrive, it being Sunday an' all.

It is a town that I'm sure could look very pretty but today no-one is in their cars. They're all parked by the roadside which makes taking an interesting photograph a frustrating challenge.

Since I am in the habit of arriving during siesta time, I find a table outside a café in the Plaza and sip white wine and munch crisps. This practice has become my post-ride staple. I am pleased with the days work. There is a little breeze and only a few tourists wander the streets. Then, as if someone had opened one vast starting gate at 5pm, the cafés fill with the jabber to which I have become accustomed, and the Plaza springs to life. Siesta is over, time to start some serious chatter. Let's get the evening started!

I left Aguilar facing another longish ride for the day, but it would see me reach the north coast and be the end, almost, of my journey, save for when I have a boat to catch. I feel that there is something of an unreal sentiment about it all.

I planned to go through the Parque Natural Saja-Besaya into Cantabria, for the scenery and greenery, and then roll into Comillas in the seaside sunshine.

There are the two main mountain ranges that run through the park at this point, and during the first 25 miles, I would climb them both. The

morning is clear and though overcast, not too chilly. Spain has been experiencing some freak storms in recent days and though they are not predicted for the north coast, rain is, and I am hoping that I am far enough west to miss it. The clouds are heavy and foreboding, but the sun fights its way through and my worries lift a little, whilst I keep an eye on the grey clouds on the horizon.

I pull into a small local garage for water and provisions, An old man shows a curious interest as he sticks his head out of the shop door whilst I dismount. He mumbles something to his colleague inside and I think I note a sly smirk. Once inside, he starts to josh with me, the garage owner grinning. I am wearing my shorts in the orange and black colours of the Spanish cycling team, Euskaltel Euskadi, which I thought would make for a talking point in the north since the team come from the Basque country. He points to them but I don't catch what he says. I tell him my line and he grins back. As I forage for my water and sugar sweets, I am frustrated by locks on all the product cabinets, which is odd, but you know there has to be a reason. The garage owner laughs and I turn and smile.

In an elaborate demonstration of pointing, waving and broken Spanish I get, in the end, that they lock everything up, he says, so that their Basque country neighbours can't come and steal everything. We all have a hearty chortle and I tell them that I just like wearing orange, the predominant colour of the team. I thought any discussion concerning the form of Sammy Sanchez, star of the Basque team, would be too much for all of us.

Back on the road, I'm quickly into the first real climb and though I pass through some interesting little places - Branosera looks pretty - I feel the need to press on. It's too early on a long climbing day to start taking pictures. I reach the top of the first climb, and because there is no breeze and the cloud cover thick, it is pleasantly warm. The whole region is lush and green with picturesque hamlets waiting for the summer tourist season.

However, heading down the other side of the mountain is a different matter. It is bitterly cold as I freewheel downhill. I seriously think about stopping at the bottom and pulling on a t-shirt underneath my top. But the sun comes out and warms my back and I change my mind. I know I'm just going to get hotter climbing.

I climb the second mountain range, taking in the sunshine and the views, glad that I didn't put another layer on after all. This is like the Lake District without the lakes... and then the fun starts.

The hillsides are mainly open allowing cattle to roam freely as they wish. I had seen Daisy climb through a roadside fence, such as they are, ahead of me, tempting her calf to follow. Calf had given up too quickly and Daisy, after a few grumps, which must have been cow for 'wimp', turned around and went back down the hillside. All this happens as I claw in the incline at a steady 4 mph. Around the bend, however, I suddenly have to start doing some thinking. Ahead of me straddling the road is a ménage a trois - a big beast I quickly determine is a bull hanging out with a couple of his girlfriends.

I approach slowly, whilst I figure out how to navigate this most unlikely of scenarios for a cyclist. There is a small roadside fence, for what it's worth, which has regular gaps to allow the cattle back and forth. As luck would have it, the girlfriends decide to walk along the grassy ledge, while Bully saunters up the road leaving a slight gap. Dare I chance to run for it?

I opt for waiting and zigzag as slowly as I can so as not to startle him. My mind calculating my chances in a downhill charge, or even an uphill one. The girls seem happy on the hillside, but when one of them begins to think for herself and head back to the pasture, Bully decides it would be best to follow his lady love and shuffles to the verge. This was my chance. You would be amazed at how fast you can overtake a bull after you have already climbed 3000 feet! I pulled ahead and toyed with the idea of stopping to take a picture. No one will believe me, I thought.

But the lady is fickle. Before I know it Bully and his girls are back on the road just a few yards behind me and, as I turn to see where he is, one of my cleats fails to disengage and I end up on my backside in the roadside mud. The girls look at me and wander to the green grass the other side of the road. Bully, stops and gazes down at me, snorts, says 'You'll never make a matador' in Bull, and follows them. Clearly other things on his mind. I dust off the worst of the mud and check that no-one is watching. Onwards.

I start my descent, gawping at the amazing scenery, trouble free. I know that from here the main work is done, though there is probably another 30 miles to go, most of it downhill or flat. Then I suddenly realise that the cloud is coming down the mountain and

that I am above it.

I pull on my wind cheater, put my lights on, and head on down. Visibility shrinks to about 10 yards, cows and horses wander or sit on the road amongst their frequent fresh droppings, and the temperature quickly drops to about 2 degrees.

You could see this farmhouse clearly just seconds before this picture was taken

Descending seems to take forever. I feel a real chill and after a while begin to shiver. I can't freewheel quickly because I can't see far enough and freewheeling is no good when it is cold. I spin my legs to try to keep the muscles warm. The cloud and mist go on and on and, as if it couldn't get any worse, it started spitting. The spit soon becomes a downpour and the only thing to focus on is to stay upright and get to my destination. Nothing else matters.

As I hit the valley floor, the rain stops for a while. I'm soaked to the skin but the air is not as cold. When the rain does return, I just need to plough on to my warm shower, avoid the white lines and make sure that I stay on the bike.

Finally, after a couple of hours or more of this, I cruise into Comillas. The rain stops and I have made it. I stood on the beach in Malaga and now I stand on the beach in Comillas. Mediterranean to the Atlantic.

I have a boat to catch on Wednesday, which is 30 more miles of riding but I'm here, dirty, tired and cold. The rain a fitting coda to 3 weeks of sunshine. Now, I hope I have a sea view...

Comillas has a very popular and beautiful sweeping beach, where you can dip your toes in the Atlantic Ocean, and boasts some fine architecture which includes the Sobrellano Palace Chapel and the Pontifical University. The University being on view as you cycle down into town.

For me, however, first prize goes to El Capricho, the first experimental design by that great, and distinctly whacky architect, Antoni Gaudí. If you have been to Barcelona you will have seen the amazing Gaudí house where nothing is as it seems and there's hardly a straight line anywhere - and then, of course,

there's the Cathedral, La Sagrada Familia. El Capricho is where it all began and where Antoni began to spread his wings.

Built between 1883 and 1885, you may be surprised to find that it isn't actually very big. But size isn't everything. This building is exquisite. From the sunflower tiles to the minaret tower, the glass roofed dining room, to the pristine finery of the woodworked attic, this house, built for a music lover and scholar, is a testament to decadence and self-indulgence.

Clearly the work of a genius.

And so to catch my boat home. It was a chilly and uneventful ride from Comillas to Santander, except that Santander was very busy, which I expected, it being a port town.

With a mixture of emotions my first solo ride crossing Spain was over. I had been so focused on this project since the middle of January, with training, planning routes and schedules and all the other stuff that goes with international travel. I knew I would miss getting up in the morning, pulling on my gear and setting off on my next leg of the journey.

I found the Spanish people invariably charming, helpful and often amusing and fun. Tolerant of my broken Spanish, we communicated and, when we both got the joke, laughed together too. I didn't mind laughing at myself, I'm sure. I found some wonderful new places to revisit and discovered parts of Spain that I would have dismissed if I had been whipping by on the Autovia.

For stat fans, I cycled 728 miles, burnt up 37,200 calories and ate the same in bread and pastry. I climbed up (and rode down) 42,880 feet, and spent almost exactly 71 hours in the saddle.

And I finish the ride with a sense of elation and expectation.

Experiences such as these introduce you to yourself no matter how old you. The more I take on different tasks and experiences, the more I learn about myself. One thing is for sure - I have been consumed by my journey, and I can't wait to start the next challenge.

Ride 2
Santiago - Belmonte - Cuenca - Burgos - Santander

		Miles
Day 1	Santiago de la Ribera to Cieza	60
Day 2	Cieza to Albacete	64
Day 3	Albacete to Belmonte	68
Day 4	Belmonte to Cuenca	61
Day 5	Cuenca rest day	
Day 6	Cuenca to Budia	69
Day 7	Budia to Siguenza	
Day 8	Siguenza to El Burgo de Osma	57
Day 9	El Burgo to Aranda	36
Day 10	Aranda to Burgos	65
Day 11	Burgos rest day	
Day 12	Burgos rest day	
Day 13	Burgos to El Ribero	66
Day 14	El Ribero to Laredo	35
Day 15	Laredo rest day	
Day 16	Laredo to Santander	40
		671

Before we begin

Have you ever had the feeling that you are not quite in control of things? 'Why, surely', you respond. I had felt for a while that the preparation for this ride hadn't been as focused as it possibly should have been, though I couldn't put my finger on the reason why. I just had an uneasy feeling that somehow not everything was pinned down.

Matters began to slide when, with six days to take-off, my new bike succumbed to a gearing problem. Though I had been riding it for a few months, I had naively placed my faith in its shiny newness. I stayed calm. I could get this fixed. Several Sunday phone calls ensured that Monday would get a result and so it was. However, a discussion with the bike repair man opened up another worrying dilemma. He expressed some concern regarding the attachment of my pannier rack, which he felt wasn't as secure as it probably should be. We agreed I needed to correct it. This meant that I needed to get at least one more ride in to ensure that the new pannier rack fitting worked satisfactorily. Cue two days of torrential rain.

Now I was beginning to stress. I couldn't realistically go to Spain without a trial ride of the new luggage compartment and time was running out.

The only thing to do was to go with my old bike. But, I hadn't ridden that for six months. Fingers crossed. The odds must be better than cycling 700 miles on my untried bike.

Wednesday and the second day of torrential rain. I checked into my garage to pack my old bike into the box. I'm sure it grinned at me. 'Hi, old friend,' I fancy it said, 'I knew you'd need me.' To my horror the incessant rain had been soaking under the garage door, and then rising like a bath-tub scum mark up the sides of my cardboard bike box, rendering it a useless heap of soggy paper. This was challenging. (See how calmly I approached this?) I could be boxless with two days to go to my flight. Throwing up my hands in despair (actually it was probably more verbal than that), I felt buffeted by the winds of ill-fortune, let alone the rain outside. By some fluke, and as a result of some previously questionable decision making, I had ended up with two boxes. One was sturdier than the other, although 'the other' had been my first choice. That one was now a wet pile of mush.

The sturdier box was still soaking up rain but offering up some resistance. In a panic, I yanked it into the hallway. There was a momentary blip on the National Grid as I crouched, hair-dryer in hand, desperately attempting to save the day.

A tense 36 hours later, after a sleepless night, I had a 4.00am start. I made the plane with five minutes to spare. I was last to board, my bike box resting on top of everyone else's luggage. I had made it by the skin of my teeth. I crashed into my Spanish hotel at 10.00am exhausted, and promptly went to bed. I had some serious battery charging to do.

"Homage to the Tormented Cyclist" on Santiago beach

Sunday morning. Santiago de la Ribera, a coastal resort lapping the shores of south eastern Spain, stretches stiff limbs and wakes slowly to a pale, whiskery Englishman assembling a bicycle on the corner of the street by the community recycling bins. He is stripped to the waist. It is 10.30am and already hot. I just could not believe it. Failing to spot minute fragments of glass, probably the aftermath of a balmy drunken night, I punctured a tyre reassembling my bike by the roadside! Then, with puncture repaired and the wheel back in place I discovered that the brakes were binding. 'Enough! Enough!', I cried. 'Ye gods of cycling. Leave me alone.' Was that three things that had gone wrong? Or was I into my second set of three? I'd lost count. There was nothing to do but keep on keeping on. Two and half hours later, and with some heavy sighs of relief, we are ready to roll...and I hoped that that was the end of it.

Tomorrow we ride!

1 Santiago de la Ribera to Belmonte

The slumbering yachts of the bay reflected in the mirror finish of the waters as I tucked into breakfast. Not even a wisp of wind to ruffle my flowing locks. Breakfast was later than I would have liked for Day 1, but there was nothing I could do but go with the flow. My plan was to shadow the main motorway north out of Santiago de la Ribera and then veer away and head directly into the city of Murcia. This was fine except that the service road running with the motorway was basically a pitted gravel track and not the smooth surface I was hoping for. This made a late start into a much later arrival into Murcia, since covering the first 10 miles of the morning was hard work. I had hoped to be through the other side of the city by lunchtime but it didn't work out that way.

Murcia seemed to be a pleasant city, certainly the centre looked charming. However, the only way for me to navigate the city centre was on foot, dodging lunchtime shoppers, and dropping on and off the cycle path, which appeared and disappeared without warning. The city conurbations seemed to go on further than I had bargained for too. The industrial zone north of the city stretched for miles and dumped me unceremoniously into a maelstrom of impatient traffic.

For refreshment and sustenance, I have developed a habit of fine dining at the Repsol restaurant in town or sometimes out of it. Things normally go well. I can manage the food and drink basics pretty easily by now. However, my experience leaving Murcia took me into uncharted territory. The expression on the attendant's face slipped seamlessly from one of pleasant welcome to that of deep frustration as he gunned the impressive range of snacking products with his finger. I followed his flashing directions, whilst trying to compute what he was telling me. His explanation, far too fast for ears and brain to connect. I was suddenly lost in the apparent complexity of buying a sandwich. My Spanish not quite good enough to enter the Meal Deal zone.

My route was taking me through the industrial dormitory towns north of the city, which are, sad to say, now fractured totems to the Spanish construction industry crash. Symbols of hope attempting to outface reality. I was not surprised by this. I've seen it elsewhere. But it is still a very sad sight to see.

I was well behind schedule by now and glad to be leaving the industrial landscape for the rugged hillsides of the Valle de Ricote. This is why I

come here. The Valle de Ricote was one of the early Moorish enclaves, between the 8th and 13th centuries, and is fed by the waters of the Rio Segura, which winds its way to Murcia city heading south. The road hugs the lower hillside wending its way through lemon, orange and peach groves cradled in the valley, the dramatic escarpments bouncing the sun onto the readily warming faces of the fruit. Spain, all is forgiven...already.

I cycled the ups and downs and twists and turns in enchantment, though I was becoming increasingly hot and tired. Cieza, my bed for the night, is a neat little place, with a nod to that European wackiness I love so much. The main "promenade" through town is decorated with tiled pillars of abstract art with paving to match. I loved it. Unfortunately, my search for a relaxing beer was stymied by the profusion of heladeria and yogurt shops. It would seem that a good night out in Cieza is getting drunk on rum and raison ice cream and taking home a healthy breakfast.

I sat awaiting my carbohydrate hit, pizza, under the awnings of a restaurant, when the peace of the evening was shattered by an almighty row between a couple who had been strolling the 'prom'. Clearly they'd had too much rum and raison. Not well versed in Spanish profanity, I could only watch in wonder. It was indeed, impossible to ignore, and serious enough to stop the traffic. Horns tooted and drivers left cars, I think in a call for calm, whilst nervous passers-by dared to step forward in case they were needed to break it up. I have never seen traffic stop to prevent pedestrians arguing. Suddenly it was all over as abruptly as it had started. No-one was hurt. Quiet descended once more and the couple shrugged off in opposite directions.

I made an early start the following morning and set my stall out to maintain a 10mph pace. It might not sound much, but as any snail will tell you, when you've got your house on your back, it's a smartish lick. Next stop Albacete. I soon pass a sign which states 'Albacete 92' . I run through the timings in my head, counting down the kilometres, visioning them fall in 10's once the sign reads 'Albacete 50'.

As a rhythm sets in, I realise that I am ahead of schedule and feeling quite pleased with myself. I take in the scenery. The morning is warm and the air fresh. Life is good. I am pootling along in my own world when up beside comes another cyclist. We chat for a short while about what we were doing, where we were going, how far we were riding today and we wish each other well. With a smile and a 'Buen Viaje' my new friend pulls ahead to leave me to trundle at my own pace. It was as he pulled ahead of me that I noticed that he had a rather strange cycling action, almost over emphasising the movement and the effort of

61

pedalling. I was stunned to see, as the distance between us quickly grew, that the strange action was due to him only having one leg, and that his action was to enable some increase in speed since we were slowly climbing. I admit I felt a burst of admiration for the young man. Followed quickly by self-admonishment. I'll never complain about achey legs again. I have two. Shut up legs, as Jens Voigt[5] would say.

The topography of the ride was akin to a ruffled carpet. Sometimes it's a gentle up-ness, sometimes a gentle down-ness. The trick is not to get suckered into thinking that your gentle up-ness is just another 'quicky', because the eyes can be deceived and you'll be slowing down before you know it. The fun thing, it turned out, was that at the 40 mile point the gentle down-ness just kept on going and going. I must have maintained an average of 18 to 20 miles an hour for the last hour since having attained a good speed it was easy to maintain with the oh, so subtle, gentle down-ness. What fun! If only it was always like that.

In December 1937, a young, naive and principled Laurie Lee re-entered Spain to confer his slight frame to the international cause in the Spanish Civil War. He recounts his experiences in his book "A Moment of War" (Penguin Modern Classics - 1991). All did not go to plan, and he found himself a prisoner of the Republic, accused of being a spy and Fascist sympathiser, in cells near Albacete station. It was, he says, a cold, snowy, 'freezing slum'.

As I arrive, Albacete is slipping into its siesta. It reminds me of Leeds, in Yorkshire, if you need a marker. To capture some of its finest charms you have to look upwards at the old, now gleaming, facades and

---

5 Jens Voigt was a German professional cyclist who retired from competition in 2014. He famously had "Shut up Legs" painted on his bike and now markets a sportswear brand called the same.

architecture. These buildings have survived the ravages of time with grace and pride. There are spacious streets, greenery, swanky shops, and a cool vibe. The young and hip populate the street side cafes, smoking and sipping coffee. Oddly, I am struck by the lack of litter. After a wash and brush up, I brave the bustle to find a table in the Main Plaza between some screaming kids and an angle-grinder. I should have noticed the waiter wearing ear defenders. But who should complain? The children are happy and there is work to be done. Do my legs ache? No, no, no they don't!

The transition from Albacete to Belmonte was one of those rides you just have to do sometimes. At the risk of sounding like a bore at the office party, I followed the N-301, which, if you care to check, is almost arrow straight for about 60 miles. Unbelievable. That's it. There was an occasional kink in and out of a small town but on and on it goes taking the region's produce to Madrid.

To paraphrase Rudyard Kipling[6], he travels the fastest who travels alone. However, even Kipling didn't venture to wonder at what goes through the mind of someone travelling alone on a dead straight road with little stimulation other than the never ending white line.

There are times, of course, when tumbleweed can be heard blowing between my ears. One leg spinning alternately to the other. I might see a fetchingly painted gantry ahead and promise myself, as a reward upon reaching it, half a banana, or 3 jelly babies. 'Go on, Al, you've worked hard. You're ahead of schedule, have both.' Or, I begin to think about my legs or my backside aching. I know. It's riveting stuff. But I knew when I planned the journey that the first three days would be spent getting through urbanisation to the interesting parts.

Yesterday's weather forecast had predicted thunderstorms, which didn't arrive so I was confident that today's forecast would be equally speculative. Heading toward Belmonte, the sun shone gloriously and I was looking forward to my first refreshment.

All was well until I looked to the north to see Armageddon bearing down on me. Indigo clouds dumping grey blue sheets in the distance. Suddenly the race was on to make it to the hotel before the thunderstorm came. I assumed a sprinter's position and pedalled like hell, finally pulling up to the front door as the rumble darkened above me.

---

[6] Rudyard Kipling,"The Winners"

Belmonte is a staging post along the Ruta del Quixote[7], 'Quixote's Road', and the Donkey Don is never far away from these parts, which is also well known for its 15th century castle. For me, emulating no-one in particular, it marks the start of the Ruta del Interest.

I wandered aimlessly in the clear, crisp, post storm air, the sun back in its proper place, and reflected. This is why I come here. A quiet, peaceful Spanish village, with history seeping out of the ground. Fittingly, there are windmills strutting the skyline and in the quiet of a sleepy afternoon I am transported to another world.

[7] From "The Ingenious Nobleman Sir Quixote of La Mancha" by Miguel de Cervantes Saavedra.

2 Belmonte to Cuenca, the Rio Júcar region.

I realise that the last of my long rides for the week is going to be slower than the others and so I am up with the donkey and raring to go. However, I am somewhat thwarted by breakfast not being served until 8, when I was hoping for 7. The Night Manager is coming to the end of his shift and offers to make me tea, explaining that his colleague has gone for bread. How can you be cross when you are faced with such charming honesty? I accept his offer. As I sit on the terraza sipping early morning tea, the sun stretches into the clear blue and I realise that life is telling me to "Cool it. Chill out, man". Sometimes you just need to be told.

I set out and the roadside poppies are bright and fresh. Spain's national flower should be the poppy. It is, in fact, the carnation, but given that poppies are everywhere they brighten the landscape with waves of smile inducing vibrant crimson.

I am riding through the region of Castilla la Mancha, described as one of Spain's least populated regions, and a region obviously famous for the great Cervantes classic.

Given the plateau and the windswept nature of the landscape, I rather naively expected more windmills. However, despite repeatedly passing signs that tell me that I am on the Ruta del Quixote, there aren't that many windmills to be tilted at, I can tell you.

The Rio Júcar meanders its way through this region for about 500 kilometres. The area is probably best explored by car, given that there is so much countryside to enjoy, especially the Júcar Canyon, with its exquisite villages and breathtaking views.

As I ride through a forest whose lush greenery is fed by the river, the escarpments become magical transformations, like rock clouds. Faces, animals and crazy shapes appear from the pitted sandstone cliffs. It's a land of mythical creatures and after-dark fairy tales.

And so, at last, Cuenca. I arrive at 5pm and have been cycling all day. I think I'll treat myself to another jelly baby or two. A UNESCO World Heritage Site that just had to be visited. It is a city of two very different characteristics. Growing up, and supporting the old town which attracts the tourists, is the modern city, now dwarfing the main attraction. The old town is simply a special place of charm and ancient streets.

This is the town where the houses are built into the rocks, Las Casas Colgadas. For the life of me, I can't imagine the thought that went into building such a stupendous cathedral when everyone around must have been steeped in poverty. The cathedral, of course, is for us to enjoy. I visited the Cathedral in the morning when the sun was behind it and then again in early evening. Appreciating the changing light, I was struck by the thought that it would make the perfect subject for a

series of paintings, as Monet did with Rouen Cathedral, reflecting the shifting impact of the sun. Its huge rusted doors and pencil columns casting different aspects as the sun swings through its arc.

The town was founded by the Moors as a defensive town, at the confluence of the Huecar and Júcar rivers, and its name derives from the Arabic 'kunka' - for 'fortress'. The 'rock' houses lining the gorge have now largely disappeared, though a couple remain hanging precipitously from the cliff face. A town of mixed fortunes throughout the centuries, rejuvenating its economy in the 20th century by focusing on tourism with justifiable cause.

Cuenca has seen a plethora of cultural festivals, but what Cuencans didn't realise was that a little known British cyclist was in town, who created an art installation on a park bench called 'Cyclist dries his smalls and other items'. This unique piece of guerrilla art lasted just for a couple of hours, but was cemented in the minds of at least three of the passers-by who saw it. Their lives will never be the same. Pictures are available, but this is a family book.

3 Cuenca to Burgos

I'd had a thoroughly enjoyable ride for the most part. Sun, blue sky, beautiful countryside, smooth road, and speed fun. I passed by the Embalse de Entrepeñas, which struck me as being worryingly low for this time of year. The Embalse is fed by the Rio Tagus. However, irrigation demands have dramatically reduced the water level in recent years and since my visit the situation has worsened considerably.

As my ride wore on, the sun became increasingly searing. I kept thinking that I was closer to Budia than I actually was and I was beginning to run out of water. The last third of the ride became a delicate balance of long slow hills, the heat and my lack of hydration. Eventually, I took to using some of the energy gels I was carrying as a source of fluid. Hills I was used to, but I was concerned about hydration in such heat and began to gently pace myself. At last, after 70 miles, I sloped in to Budia to the sound of 'Jumping Jack Flash'. It couldn't have been me they were referring to, could it?

This has to be the noisiest village I have ever experienced. I arrive into the Plaza de España at 4.00pm to find this sleepy mountain village blasting out The Rolling Stones from the local bar and two gentlemen, clearly the worse for a lunchtime session, sitting by the doorway drinking and shouting at each other in an amiable 'I can shout louder than you' challenge. This unashamed musical preference and opinion sharing continues whilst I get my bearings and size up my surroundings. And it goes on... and on. I spruced up and wandered the empty streets to the clamorous sound of a heavy metal band ricocheting from the stonework like some urchin hunting Frankenstein. The shouty gents had moved on to something far more inane, yet twice as loud.

My host in Budia recommended a restaurant for dinner, which unfortunately won't open until much later. This is a regular challenge in cycling through Spain. Spanish eating patterns don't tend to coincide with the requirements of the hungry cyclist after a long ride, when dinner early, bed and rise early, is preferred. Nevertheless, the bar is open and I take a table on the small terraza. There are two card schools of Budian gentry in full swing, one for money and one for honour, dealing and bidding...and shouting at each other. One chap in particular dominates the exchanges with the booming tones of a "Harry Secombe"[8]. Downstairs, the restaurant has been hired for a private party for the afternoon and the disco is still going. There is football on the bar tv. I consider rolling a paper napkin into ear plugs.

Budia rooftops

The stranger in town is trying his best to mind his own business, tapping away on his iPad, with a thoughtful landlady bringing me the wi-fi password on a piece of paper. Clearly she sees that I might need to connect to the outside world to reassure my kin that despite all, I am still alive.

Meanwhile, Spanish Harry Secombe, even bearing a faint resemblance, is in full flow and I am left to wonder how he courted his lady love. Did he whisper sweet nothings or does she now suffer from hearing loss and enjoys the silencio?

Surprisingly, there is a Tourist Office, next door to the Rolling Stones bar, which opens for an hour in the evening. I am greeted as if I was the only customer that day, and probably I was. I tell the friendly official that I am English and that if he speaks too quickly I won't be able to follow

---

8 Welsh tenor and comedian.

him. This doesn't deter him, however, and after inviting me into the Peasant House mock-up, and delighting in showing me the handheld urinal that slides under the bed, I leave having been given several kilos of information leaflets. I demonstrate the stress of my load by buckling at the knees but he just laughs. Another unsuspecting tourist sent on his way with the answers to everything.

Presently dinner is served to the sound of the football on tv. I shouldn't complain - at least they fed me. And would you know it, silence descends like a mist around midnight and Wee Willy Winky has ushered everyone to bed.

All too soon the sun rises and the church bell tolls its timely reminder of daybreak, as it has done every 15 minutes since 6am. Budia stretches and yawns. Somewhere, in a matchbox bedroom in a house grand with time, in a street paved with stories, Spanish Harry Secombe is awakened and strokes the familiar softness of his wife's shoulders as she lay, her back turned toward him. 'It is Sunday, my love. You know Sunday is our day,' he bellows, as softly as he can. His wife flinches away with a grouch, reaches for that which has become her comforting companion in her later years, her ear-trumpet, and grips it with the eager hand-shake of a long lost friend. She may slumber, but her arm is swift, and the ear-trumpet cracks Mr. Spanish Harry Secombe across his hand.

'I've a headache...and it is your fault', she said.

Meanwhile, out on the road, a pair of white legs spin in hope of a sun-tan.

Having checked my route the previous evening, I knew that my road north met an A road motorway and was blocked off to go no further. Thereby, of course, ceasing my progress too. However, by the wonders of Google Earth I had discovered a track, about a mile long, which if I could access it, could save myself a serious diversion. I decided to gamble and go for it. I was banking on the fact that the Spanish farmer wouldn't allow such simple access to be cut off and thus force themselves into countless extra miles. If my gamble failed, I would add a couple more hours of cycling to my day. The day had become cold and very windy by the time I reached the start of the track. But I was buoyed by seeing my gamble pay off. Clever farmers. My hunch was right. Let it rain.

I have begun to think that no self-respecting Spanish town should be without a castle. There are, of course, some superb castles throughout the country in the major tourist spots but even on a trip like this you will come across less imposing castles of interest. The castle on the hill at Siguenza is my bed for the knight. I head for the hilltop castle of Atienza the following day and then on to El Burgo de Osma and its ruined castle. A hat trick without trying.

Atienza

I had highlighted a serious climb indeed, about halfway through the journey to El Burgo de Osma, and it was important to fuel up for this if I was going to give it my best shot. As I approached Miedes de Atienza, the hills rose in the distance, a thin grey stripe cleaving the range. I was heading for the Castilla y Leon line.

The Paso de Ganado is a long snaking climb out of the valley to the tops of the moors, and as is the nature of long snaking climbs, facilitates fantastic views at every sweeping bend. As I reached the moorland summit I couldn't believe my luck. On top of the moors, surprisingly, there wasn't a breath of wind, and the views stretched unblemished for miles into the distance.

Only the sleepiest cyclist can take the wrong direction out of the smallest town. And then, due to some motorway access restrictions, add to his woes by having to pursue an eight mile detour. What had been an N road when planning the trip had, in the meantime, been upgraded to a blue A road section and I was banned. I had decided to scoot down the main highway and get on with it. However, this was not to be.

So it was that on leaving El Burgo de Osma, 'burgo' relates to the English word 'borough', I found myself attempting to navigate my way around Alcubilla de Marques, a tiny hamlet on the Camino del Cid. This Camino runs from the northwest to the south east and follows the journey of Rodrigo Díaz de Vivar, El Cid Campeador. I checked my map and spotted that a road through Alcubilla seemed to end about a mile from another opportunity to join the road westward. Having had some success with my previous hunch,

wine stores at Alcubilla de Marques

I dared to try again.

Alas, one hunch too many and my faith in hunches came to nothing. I found myself back tracking to try another route. However, the fun of exploring is always done in the small villages and I came across more wineries cut into the hillside under the conical hill that marks the village.

I suspect Aranda must suffer from being the town that everybody drives past on the way to Madrid. The tourists having "done" Burgos, now, a couple of hours lazy drive, Madrid.

I had promised myself that at some point I would experience that most Spanish of passions - the bull fight. Though I admit I had been dodging the issue, since I knew I wouldn't feel comfortable. I'm not happy with the baiting of animals, whether it be bull fights or the chasing of foxes by packs of dogs and people on horseback. Admittedly, in all the towns that I had stayed in so far, the bullrings had remained closed. My hotel in Aranda is actually adjacent to the bullring. But still the bullring is closed. All cultures are multi-faceted. Centuries of history spawn myths, legends and ceremonies. Spain and bull-fighting go hand-in-glove. I felt it important to experience something of the lore and tradition of this passionate country besides its castles and windmills. I had glimpsed bullfights on the ubiquitous tv screens in bars across the country but had averted my eyes, fearful of my reaction. However, if I was going to experience it in any way, tv seemed the safest. For me, at least.

As much as anything I was interested in the reaction of the people. Matadors are well trained and the outcome largely predictable. (Only two matadors have been killed by bulls since 1985. The last one being Ivan Faniño in 2017 while fighting in France.) There are three stages to a bull fight and the presence of several banderillas, coloured lances, hanging from the animal's neck signals that I am joining the event near the end of Stage 2. The spectators in the ring seemed to be enjoying themselves. Chatting and grinning in the sunshine. In the bar, though there were many customers, few paid the tv any heed. I began to feel conspicuous in my concentration. The final thrust, the bull is floored and swiftly relieved of its suffering. Its carcass dragged away. A bow by the matador and I leave. The final whistle blown. The live screening was enough for me. I have been blooded.

As you would imagine in these enlightened times, any discussion around bullfighting raises passions on both sides of the debate. My experience in a daytime bar crowd may not be typical but perhaps it does suggest a fading desire for the tragic version of the spectacle. The sword is now being replaced by other spectacular alternatives such as the 'recortadores', who face the bull solely with their wits and agility, swerving, diving and jumping to safety. I shall have to track down a 'recorte' on my next trip.

As previously, I am riding in May before the tourist season opens in June, and as a consequence must grab food on the road where I can, and yes, theoretically, it's not scientifically endorsed. For instance, here, is what constitutes ride fuel.

I can get two days cycling out of these. The donuts are sugar bombs and if I really want to fuel the machine with a toxic load then I have been known to throw in a couple of jelly babies. Donut with a jelly baby top and I'm a rolling ball of sugar, babe. Singing silly songs in my head - not a care in the world.

Whilst we pause for reflection, here are a few reasons that come to mind, why cycling through Spain is so enjoyable. In no particular order, as they say;

* The countryside is beautiful and the old villages ultimately charming and fascinating and … I love photographing faded glory of old villages.

* The People. In cycling through Spain I've never met anyone who isn't helpful.

* In mountain villages everyone says 'Hola' to the stranger, and the camaraderie between fellow travellers with a wave, shout, or even chat on the road, is heartwarming.

* The almost ubiquitous cycle lanes.

* The traffic gives cyclists respect.

* The road surfaces - usually smooth as a baby's bum.

* The sunshine. You don't have to race to where you are going. The chances are it's going to be fine all day. Except, of course, when in the north of the country where you might need an extra layer in the morning.

* Solomillo. A beef steak in all its varieties. Sorry veggies, it is a prize after a hard ride and a protein hit.

* And lastly, the challenge. It really is a great way to see the country.

The main route from Aranda to Burgos is straight as an arrow, and I suspect, the route most people will take. However, if you are cycling, you almost certainly have to choose the scenic route through the villages. Zigzagging your way through the countryside is much longer but far more agreeable. I planned my route over a post-bullfight glass of wine, scraps of paper and pencil in hand, listing the villages in order until I reached Burgos. First village x then on to y and so on. This is real Ribera del Duero country with some fancy wineries flirting with the lonely traveller. Unfortunately, no time to stop.

The scenery, of course, is stunning and the further north I go the greener it becomes.The zigzag route often finds me in the middle of nowhere, and I manage to find the right road from Cilleruelo, a tiny hamlet, to Villafruela, a small village, via a stark stretch of moorland. Midday was approaching and I was the only moving object for miles, apart from, that is, a road repair gang who were diligently filling in potholes before the heat of the day really kicked in.

The gang leader, clad head to toe in green overalls, waved her clipboard at me as I approached. What is a cyclist doing along here? Or maybe it was a slow day - filling in potholes - and she just wanted to talk ? Her questions came at me gunfire fast, as foreign languages always seem to be to the ears of a non-native, but I'd been here a couple of weeks and my 'ear' was becoming attuned to catch the gist at least. That said, she was clearly wondering what on earth I was doing in the middle of nowhere and where I was headed.

'Villafruela,' I said, 'is it okay?'

'Si, si, ocho kilometres,' she said,…and then something else

I repeated 'ocho kilometres'. It's a good ruse for buying time if you can grasp something coming at you and repeat it. After a few more questions to assuage her incredulity, she wished me 'buen viaje' and waved me off to slalom wet puddles of tarmac for the next 5 miles. I arrived at a junction into Villafruela with no signposts and only a one in three chance of getting my next move right. And it was here that I met the unsuspecting old lady whose directional skills with my poor Spanish begins the book. Working on another hunch, I guessed correctly and I was on my way to Burgos. On the Hunchometer I had two out of three right on this trip. I was beginning to feel like a proper explorer.

…The iglesia of Iglesiarubia fame…

Not only is Burgos a beautiful city, but I have managed to arrive the

day before La Noche Blanca, the White Night, which celebrates all things cultural, but mainly musical it seems, that the city has to offer.

Although much of the festivities during my visit is punctuated by heavy downpours, nothing dampens the spirits of the many performers and street musicians who entertain on every corner.

Some are dressed in medieval garb, others in 'team' colours. A troupe of Indian dancers drum and twirl their way through the city. Acrobats spin suspended from a crane. The celebration is everywhere and the vibe is eclectic.

The highlight for me is the gothic cathedral of Saint Mary. Begun in the 13th century and expanded and adapted through the ages, this building is truly stunning.

I spent hours here marvelling at the plaster work, the art, the wooden carvings and frescoed chapels. An unforgettable experience.

Given Spain's troubled past during the 20th century, I sometimes marvel at how these buildings have survived but remain grateful that they have. They provide a welcome pause in a hectic modern life.

4 Burgos to Laredo

Burgos had provided a cultural highlight but it was time to focus on reaching the sea. Tapas, that little something with your drink, seems to me to be so civilised. Of course, people have been eating and drinking this way for centuries in Spain. Though perhaps not quite the same way in the UK until the invention of the bag of crisps or nuts. There are several stories considering the first tapa in Spain. Whether small morsels were decreed to assist the recuperation of Alfonso X of Castille in the 13th century, or the evolution from the eating habits of peasants who needed little and often while working the land, legends abound.

I break my journey by staying in a small local castle, in a hamlet on the way to Laredo. This being the only option amongst the ten houses that make up the community. It is still early in the tourist season and the dining room is closed. However, the bar, thankfully, isn't, and is alive with local chatter, beer and tapas. Todays riding has brought on a certain hunger and the need to replenish. I ordered two tapas - patatas bravas and chorizo - figuring that that should be ample.

...The Puerto de Los Tornos...the Valle de Soba to the left and the Valle de Carranza to the right

What my charming host brings me is akin to half a sack of potatoes and a dead pig. This is a problem since my early childhood was underpinned

78

by the insistence upon clearing my plate. Such ingrained conditioning is hard to fight, isn't it? I try my best to devour the bounty but I know I'm going to fail, and I do eventually surrender. I apologise to my host for not making a better fist of it but inwardly wishing that standardisation of tapas sizes is something the EU could get their teeth into.

The route to the boat and my ferry home is through the beautiful national parks that make up the mountain range in the north. I am east of the Montaña Oriental and west of the Gorbieako Parke Naturala heading for Laredo to kick around and wait until Wednesday when my boat sails. Los Tornos is a mountain pass linking the regions of Burgos and Cantabria with some steep sections to navigate. However, having done that, the views are spectacular. Even on dull, wet days like these.

When I get there, the northern coastal town of Laredo is in limbo. The smaller independent shops in the old town are all closed. Towering beachside hotels stare at the empty sea awaiting the first of the season's visitors. The wind off the Bay of Biscay is high and wild. In the churchyard I find a monument to those who fell during Spain's Civil War. Spain continues to wrestle with this tragic period of its history and tellingly the brickwork is bare where name plaques might have been. Circumspection probably being called for when reflecting on a period that split families, towns and country. All I have to do now is to wake up on Wednesday, climb aboard one more time and catch the ferry. It all seems to have been over so quickly. I'm already thinking that I could do with another week. I feel tired in that I need a good night's sleep. A different bed almost every night is not conducive to a good rest until you get to the point of exhaustion. Then you can sleep anywhere.

...I can see the sea ...

Particularly since Belmonte, I have ridden through some gorgeous countryside and seen some wonderful old houses which have only inspired me to come back and paint some of it. The views have been consistently splendid. I have covered 1300 miles cycling Spain, enjoying its quieter corners, Budia included, as well as its magnificent cities. The one thing for sure is that I will be back. There is still more to see by bicycle. The only way. I hope you give it a go.

Adios, te veré en el camino.

Appendix 1

My packing list, to get you started...

Paperwork:
Routes - broad brush plan
Passport
Air Ticket
Ferry Ticket
Euros
Wallet/cards
Emergency Number 112
Pencil/pen
Phrasebook ?

Bike:
Tyre levers
Inner tubes x 4
Pump
Multi-tool
Allen keys
Chain repair link
Cycle Locks
Puncture repair kit
Insulated water bottles
Small scissors
Swiss knife
Oily rag
Bin liners for unpacking bike in Spain
Pannier rack
Long nose pliers
Spare Pannier fixing screws

Clothing:
T-shirts x 2
Thin extra base layer
Pants x 2
Bandana (the sun can be hot on your neck)
Cycle tops x 2
Cycle shorts x 2
Sunglasses
Helmet

Cycling sunglasses
Sandals footwear
Cut off shorts/ legs
Wind cheater/ shower proof cycling top
Light jumper for cool nights
Personal medicines if appropriate
Cycle socks x 2
Hand desanitizer
Arm warmers
Wet wipes
Clothing wash flakes

Electrics:
Garmin
Charger plug
European adaptor
Garmin cable
iPad
Apple cable
Cycle light
Rear light
Light charger
Rear light battery if necessary
Powerpack
Phone
Earphones

Food:
Gels
Bars
Instant porridge for self-catering breakfasts

Appendix 2

Accommodation

Ride 1

Malaga:	Tryp Málaga Alameda Hotel
El Burgo:	Casa Grande de El Burgo
Algodonales:	La Carrihuela
Sevilla:	Apartment in 16th courtyard - https://www.airbnb.co.uk/rooms/1585275?euid=cc876dc5-d34b-157f-bb94-6f71efd5b757
Monesterio:	Hotel Leo
Mérida:	Hotel Ilunion Mérida Palace
Cacerés:	Apartamento Villalobos - Airbnb
Plasencia:	Parador de Plasencia
Guijuelo:	Hotel Entrebos
Salamanca:	Sercotel Los Torres
Tordesillas:	Hotel Torre de Sila
Palencia:	Hotel Castilla Vieja
Aguilar de Campoo:	Hotel Valentin
Comillas:	Hotel Mar

Ride 2

Santiago de la Ribera:	Hotel Ribera
Cieza:	Hotel San Sebastián Hospederia
Albacete:	Sercotel San Jose
Belmonte:	Palacio del Infante Don Juan Manuel Hotel Spa
Cuenca:	Apartment Airbnb - Apto De Diseño en Casco Antiguo - www.airbnb.co.uk/rooms/3247612
Budia:	Apartamentos El Condor
Siguenza:	Parador de Siguenza
El Burgo de Osma:	El Balcon de la Catedral
Aranda:	Hotel Aranda
Burgos:	Apartment - Airbnb - Calle de Fernan Gonzalez 50, Burgos
El Ribero:	Palacio de los Alvarado
Laredo:	Hotel Cosmopol

Afterword

Thank you for buying this edition of "Crossing Spain". I hope you have enjoyed it, found it informative and entertaining. If you have, a review on Amazon would be appreciated and would help me greatly.

I am grateful for your support. Good luck in your travels and, if you do, your cycling.

Alan

Printed in Great Britain
by Amazon

81339574R00049